The advice and suggestions presented in this book are not intended as a substitute for qualified medical counseling. It is wise to consult a physician before undertaking any significant dietary or lifestyle changes.

RAW
FOOD

Erica Palmcrantz Aziz, Irmela Lilja

RAW FOOD

120 Dinners, Breakfasts, Snacks, Drinks, and Desserts

Photographs by Anna Hult
Translation by Alicia Rawls

Skyhorse Publishing

Contents

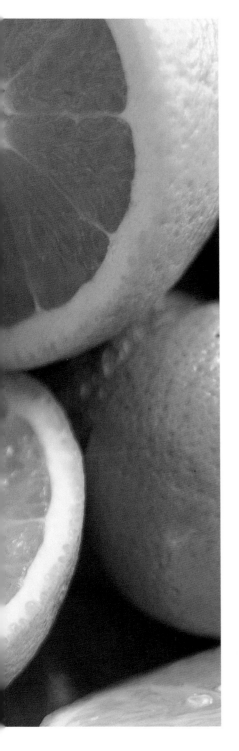

Foreword

I only met my younger cousin Erica, the author of this beautiful book, a few times when I was a child, and then not again until she visited us as an adult. What a transformation had occurred; she had blossomed into a svelte beauty! But her story was not all happy. As a teenager, she broke her back and, due to compound injuries received in a second accident, she lived in a state of chronic pain. The pain drove her to do all she could to make her body more comfortable, including regular exercise and a diet that restricted white sugar, white flour, and dairy. She worked as a personal trainer because the constant movement kept her from stiffening up. The level to which she pushed herself while working out put me to shame. I was inspired! If Erica could push past the pain to exercise with such integrity, then surely I could, too!

Erica stayed with us for three months in California and ate 100% raw vegan; she was amazed that her pain continued to lessen the longer she stayed raw. So Erica returned to Sweden on a mission to bring raw foods to this small northern country! Soon she was catering fashion shows with raw food and doing TV, magazine, and newspaper interviews. I was impressed and excited for her! But when I saw this book, I was excited for everybody; now we have a book that will inspire the world to eat a raw food diet, also called a living food diet—a diet that will bring life to you, and will bring you to life!

I lost 45 lbs. on the raw food diet just like the one outlined so simply and elegantly in this book. The diet took away a tumor, acne, candida, and depression—and that's just in me. In working as a raw vegan educator, writing about the raw diet, and receiving hundreds of emails a week from raw vegans, I have heard thousands of stories of people experiencing similar relief from so many of our society's discomforts, great and small. But it was my experiences giving birth that convinced me to go 100% raw once and for all! I have had five children, all at home, with my husband as mid-wife. For my first child, I had been eating cooked foods throughout the pregnancy, and the labor was 30 hours—and painful. For my second, I stuck to raw food, and the labor was 2 hours, and almost completely pain free. My third, I was back to cooked food, and it was 40 hours—and painful. That was enough. I wanted another delivery like the short, painless one! From then on, I stuck to raw food and my last two labors were very quick, and relatively pain free.

I so enjoy the photos of the mouthwatering nutrient-dense foods, guilt-free pleasures, and healing recipes in this un-cook book! There is nothing more beautiful than the gorgeous plants this good Earth has offered us to eat while we are her guests. And Erica, a fashion model by trade, is living proof that the raw vegan diet does a body great!

In Joy!
Jinjee Talifero
TheGardenDiet.com

Welcome

TO THE WORLD OF RAW FOOD!

The purpose of this book is to help you understand more about raw food. This book would have been an enormous help if I could have read it when I was new to raw food! Inside is an abundance of delicious recipes that contain readily available ingredients. You will probably look at fruit and vegetable dishes in a whole new way after trying these recipes! *Raw Food* was written for both complete beginners and those of you who have experience eating raw food and would like to learn more. Raw food can be incorporated into many different lifestyles, and Irmela and I have tried to illustrate this by including interviews with four people who each describe their own unique relationship to raw food. I hope this book will inspire you to find your own relationship to raw food.

As for me, I began eating raw food without really realizing it. In February of 2005 I traveled to California to visit my cousin and her family, whom I hadn't seen in twenty years. During this time in my life, I felt burned out and needed to get away, and like most of us on vacation, I ate the food that was offered to me!

The Talifero family had 90 pounds of oranges on their kitchen counter, the largest avocados I had ever seen, and a pantry entirely full of nuts. All of their meals were very simple, and the food was fantastic. I initially thought that I wouldn't become full or get enough energy from these foods, but it proved to be exactly the opposite.

After a couple of weeks I noticed that my physical problems and complaints had almost completely dissipated, and I wondered if it was because of my recent change in diet. I had previously had problems with digestion, often felt bloated, had blood sugar swings which caused moodiness, and was a little overweight. I also noticed that my attitude had changed; I had become more positive, creative and trusting.

My cousin Jinjee and her husband Storm continue to be my biggest sources of inspiration, and I am forever grateful that they gave me the opportunity to experience what raw food can do. They have five children, live on 100% raw, organic, and local food, and are well known in America within the raw food movement.

After eight weeks of eating only raw food, it was quite a challenge returning home to Sweden and trying to fit my new lifestyle into my "old" life. But I knew then that raw food had become an integral part of my life, and that it was going to continue to be. Since then, it has been quite a journey with its many ups and downs. Having an unusual lifestyle can be challenging, and standing up for how I have chosen to eat and live is not always easy. But what motivates me to continue on this path is how incredibly good I feel from eating raw, and this inspires me to share this feeling with others and help them to experience it themselves.

The recipes in this book were created in my kitchen using the ingredients that I commonly keep at home, with taste and nutrition in mind. I love good food, and I want to show you that it can be easy and fun to prepare delicious food filled with life and energy!

During my raw food journey, I met Irmela Lilja, a health and human resources journalist who is also interested in raw food. She has co-authored and contributed to the book since its inception. Exchanging ideas, discussing raw food, and collaborating with Irmela on this book has been quite rewarding.

These days I am a so-called high raw–vegan, which means that raw food makes up at least 85% of what I eat. I sometimes eat cooked food when I am a guest at someone else's home, when I want to have a snack out in a café, or during the winter months. My goal is to feel as happy and healthy as possible, which means that I choose the best available alternative for each moment.

It is important that you incorporate raw food into your life in a way that works for your daily routine. Only you can decide what is best: maybe it is enough to swap a cooked snack for fruit once a day, or maybe you want to eat only raw foods.

Raw food is more of a lifestyle than a trendy diet or a way to lose weight. When you start to eat more raw foods not only do you have more energy and vitality, but you automatically begin to choose organic foods and think more about what is good for yourself and the earth.

Go raw—your way!

—*Erica*

RAW
FOOD

Food made from fruits, berries, vegetables, seeds, nuts, dried fruits, algae, sprouts, legumes, honey, cold-pressed oil, and spices.

The ingredients are not heated above 104 degrees.

Erica Palmcrantz Aziz, 31 years old, is a raw food educator and has been a high raw–vegan for almost four years. She lives in Gothenburg, Sweden with her husband Sam Aziz and their daughter Saga, 10 months. When she's not experimenting with raw food recipes, Erica likes to spend time with her family, exercise, be out in nature, and go out with friends. For Erica, raw food is first and foremost about vitality and energy.

Erica's raw food tip: "Drinking a delicious smoothie for a snack is an easy way to get new energy."

Irmela Lilja, 49 years old, lives in Stockholm with her 14-year-old daughter Ebele. Irmela is a health and human resources journalist. She enjoys meeting family and friends, walking in the forest, traveling, yoga, dancing and working out. She eats mostly vegetarian food with a lot of raw food. "Raw food gives energy and a feeling of lightness in the body."

Irmela's raw food tip: "A homemade raw breakfast is a great way to start the day!"

Raw food—an introduction

Choose the level that is appropriate for you.

The recipes are for one person unless otherwise stated. The taste of the dishes will vary slightly depending on the size of the fruits and vegetables, whether they are organic or conventionally produced, and whether they are local or not. Use the recipes in this book as a starting point, and play around and experiment with your own recipes from there.

This introduction will tell you which ingredients and kitchen supplies you should have in your kitchen, whether you are a beginner, you want to take it a step further, or you are on your way to becoming a raw food enthusiast.

But first some important information about raw food . . .

How warm can it be and still be raw?

Warming food up to approximately 104 degrees keeps many of the nutrients in your food intact. Heating food above 104 to 115 degrees can negatively affect many of these nutrients. A fundamental thought behind eating raw is that our body receives the maximum amount of nutrients from the food we eat because it isn't exposed to high temperatures.

Frozen and raw?

Storing berries and vegetables in the freezer can also negatively impact the food's nutritional value; it also depends on which freezing method you use. The best method is to freeze the berries immediately after you have picked or bought them.

The difference between raw food and living food.

Both raw food and living food preparation consists of preparing food from fresh (and sometimes frozen or dried) vegetables, fruits, berries, seeds, nuts, or sprouts without heating them higher than approximately 104 degrees.

The difference is that living food consists of soaking, sprouting, and fermenting many of the ingredients that are used in food preparation. This is considered to be the optimal way to prepare food, as these techniques both increase the nutritional value of the food and make the ingredients easier to digest. But these preparation techniques can be too much for many of us, as they don't always easily fit into our daily routine.

Raw food is less complicated and easier to incorporate into our daily lives. Although we also soak and sprout ingredients in a raw food diet, it is most important to keep it simple and choose the best alternative for your circumstances. If you don't have the time to soak nuts, it's not the end of the world to eat them as they are! If you want to go to a café with friends, it is a step in the right direction if you choose juice (even if it is pasteurized) instead of a café latte. And if you replace your after-dinner chocolate cake or cinnamon bun with some nuts and dried fruit, you are taking a big step on the way toward a more "living" life!

Why soak?

Soaking seeds and nuts in water wakes up their life-giving properties by activating the enzymes present in the food. Soaking makes it easier to absorb the energy present in the seeds and nuts (in the form of amino acids in the proteins) and makes them easier to digest. Soaking dried fruit also aids the digestive process. Much of the sugar in the fruit is released in the soaking water, and you can save this to use as a sweetener for nut and seed milk, or use it in preparing other dishes.

Although all of the seeds, nuts and dried fruit included in the recipes of this book can be soaked, I have specified "soaked" in certain recipes where soaking is important in achieving the right consistency and texture of the dish.

How to soak:

We typically soak nuts and seeds for approximately eight hours (or overnight) and dried fruit for around 12 to 24 hours. Keep your food in the refrigerator if you soak it for more than 12 hours on a warm day.

Place the seeds, nuts or dried fruit in a plastic bowl and fill it with water (use at least three times more water than ingredients). I generally use less water for dried fruit and more water for nuts and seeds.

Why sprout?

Sprouts are extremely nutritious and are filled with living energy! In the beginning, make it easy for yourself and buy sprouts; later, you can sprout at home. It is quite rewarding to watch the little group of sprouts grow and know that you are making your own cheap and delicious food! However, it does require some planning if you want a daily supply of home-made sprouts. Sprouts should also be rinsed once a day.

> **TIP!**
> Remember to drink water when you eat seeds and nuts that you haven't soaked.

> **TIP!**
> Remember that it should be fun to sprout. If sprouting at home doesn't work, it's better just to go to the grocery store and buy ready-made sprouts without a guilty conscience!

How to sprout

More often than not, the packaging on seeds and legumes gives you information regarding soaking and sprouting times. Usually the seeds should be soaked for about eight hours (overnight) and then rinsed once a day until they are ready to be eaten. Certain sprouts, like alfalfa sprouts, grow green leaves filled with chlorophyll if you place the jar or bowl on a sunny windowsill toward the end of the sprouting process.

Check your local store to see what kind of sprouts are available where you live.

TIP!
Sprouting must be done in a cool (but not too cold) place. If you live in a warm climate, rinse seeds more often to discourage germ growth.

TIP!
Be careful with the little sprout tails when you rinse them!

Easy-to-sprout seeds, beans, and lentils:

Alfalfa seeds, mung beans, green lentils, black lentils, other small lentils (red lentils do not sprout), quinoa, and buckwheat are the easiest to sprout. The buckwheat should be peeled and whole, and it is important to rinse away the residue that accumulates when it is soaked. If you don't use special sprouting jars, you will need a quart-sized glass jar, a fine-meshed mosquito net or a cheesecloth, and a strong rubber band.

1. First, remove the damaged and discolored seeds/beans/lentils. Put the usable ones in your sprouting jar. Secure the net or cheesecloth over the jar with a rubber band. Rinse once.
2. Use half a cup of seeds, beans, or lentils to one and a half cups of water, and two tablespoons of alfalfa to one and a half cups of water when you soak. Soak the beans between six and twelve hours, and soak the seeds between four and eight hours. Remove from water after soaking.
3. Rinse the seeds, beans or lentils and let the water run out of the jar. Cover the jar, or keep it in a cupboard, as sprouts grow best in the dark.
4. Rinse with room temperature water once a day.

The sprouting time for ready-to-eat sprouts is between two to five days, except for quinoa, which will be ready after one to two days. Keep the finished sprouts in the refrigerator. They will last between two and four days.

raw food

YOUR OWN JOURNEY FROM BEGINNER TO ENTHUSIAST

It can initially feel overwhelming to introduce many new ingredients into your diet in a short period of time. However, it doesn't take too much effort or money to acquire the staple ingredients that will make it easy and convenient for you to incorporate raw food into your daily life.

1. for beginners

THE FIRST STEPS

The foundation of raw food cuisine is all of the wonderful fresh fruits and vegetables that are available. Choose organic and local produce as often as possible. Organic produce often tastes better and contains more nutrients than conventionally grown produce, so you receive more quality from less quantity! Choosing local and organic also helps protect the environment. However, it is not always possible to eat exclusively from organic and local sources so just do the best that you can.

If you live in a larger city, you can find the majority of the ingredients in the grocery store, and the remainder can be found in a natural food store. Products can of course be harder to come by depending on where you live. Natural food stores can sometimes order the products that you are looking for. It is also possible to order these products on the Internet. A good way to cut down on the shipping costs is to divide the order among friends.

INGREDIENTS

1. Almonds, Nuts, and Seeds

Nuts and seeds are rich in nutrients and there are many different kinds to choose from. Always buy raw and unsalted nuts and seeds. Store the nuts in the refrigerator so they won't go bad. Seeds give us energy, are easier to digest than nuts, and they contain less fat.

Almonds—aren't technically a nut, they are a pit from a stone fruit. Rich in nutrients.

Hazelnuts—are grown primarily in Turkey. A brown spot in the center means the nut is old. Two ounces a day of hazelnuts meets the recommended dietary allowance for vitamin E intake.

Pistachios—have a more mild taste when they aren't roasted. Raw pistachios are now commonly available in grocery stores.

Cashews—aren't really raw because the shell is steamed in order to get the nut out. But we eat them anyway, for nutrition and taste's sake.

Walnuts—have a high content of healthy omega-3 fats. They also contain tryptophan which helps calm us down when we are stressed out or upset.

Peanuts—can be found shelled and raw in most grocery stores.

Pine nuts—are the edible seeds of pine trees, from pine cones. Best known for being used in pesto sauce.

Brazil nuts—contain selenium that is hard for us to find in other foods because many soils lack sufficient selenium. The soil is rich in selenium in Brazil, where this nut primarily comes from.

Macadamia nuts—are getting easier to find raw. Compared with other nuts, they have more fat and less protein. Included in several recipes because of their soft texture and buttery flavor.

Sunflower seeds—are very versatile, and can be eaten for breakfast, dinner and dessert. Rich in polyunsaturated fats, vitamin E, calcium, potassium, iron, and zinc.

Pumpkin seeds—are rich in zinc, which helps our skin heal itself. A zinc deficiency can lead to a lowered sex drive; more pumpkin seeds in your diet can help.

Sesame seeds, light and dark—should always be bought unshelled because they are more nutritious; also, hulled sesame seeds aren't raw because they are heated in order to remove the shell. The darker sesame seeds are most nutritious but can be harder to find. Good source of healthy fats, iron and calcium.

Flax seeds, brown and gold—are rich in omega-3 and -6 fats, but they need to be ground in order for us to assimilate the fats. Do it yourself with a coffee grinder, instead of buying ground flax seeds from the store, to ensure their freshness. Flax seeds have a laxative effect. For best results, take 2 tablespoons a day.

Buckwheat, shelled and whole—is a plant, and therefore gluten free. It is rich in protein and works well as a base ingredient in vegetable and fruit salads.

2. Dried Fruit
Buy organic to ensure that the fruit hasn't been treated with sulphur.

Apricots, dried and sulfite-free—have the lowest glycemic index (GI) of all of the dried fruits, and therefore don't affect our blood sugar levels as much as other dried fruit. Rich in iron. Always choose the brown apricots.

Raisins—are commonly available, and there are many different brands and types to choose among. Avoid the raisins that are filled with preservatives.

Dried figs—should be stored in an airtight container in the pantry so they don't dry out. A good source of calcium, potassium, magnesium, and iron.

Dates, fresh or dried—are used as a sweetener in raw food dishes. There are 400 different types. Honey dates can be ordered online. Medjool dates are the large dates that you often find in grocery stores. Don't forget to take out the pits. If you use dried dates, soak them for a couple of hours before eating them.

3. Honey

Honey is rich in essential amino acids and nutrients; however, it has the same effect on blood sugar levels as regular sugar. Honey in liquid form has usually been heated. Organic honey that is firm or solid at room temperature is probably raw. If you want to be completely sure, contact the beekeeper or company who makes the honey and ask. To liquify the honey, mix it with a little lukewarm water. If you prefer not to eat honey at all, you can always substitute agave nectar (see p. 28) for honey in any of the recipes.

4. Carob/Cocoa

Carob is made from the fruit of the St. John's bread tree, which grows primarily in the Middle East. The taste is similar to cocoa, but carob contains much less fat. Roasted and raw carob powder is available in most health food stores. Raw cocoa is extremely nutritious; it contains magnesium, among other nutrients. You can buy raw cocoa and carob on the Internet.

5. Oils

Cold-pressed and organic oil, at a reasonable intake of about two tablespoons a day, is very healthy for us. Olive, canola, and flaxseed oil are particularly useful to have in your pantry.

6. Pickled Vegetables

There are different types of pickled vegetables that have been fermented, for example cabbage, carrot, or vegetable medleys. The most common is sauerkraut. Read the packaging to make sure that the vegetables haven't been pasteurized. Beneficial for our intestinal bacteria.

7. Spices and Herbs

There is a wide variety of fantastic spices—both fresh and dried—to help add flavor to our dishes. Commonly available fresh herbs include basil, parsley, thyme, dill, mint, and lemon balm. Cinnamon, cardamom, paprika, cumin, and nutmeg are just some of the dried spices that give your food a little extra oomph. Ginger is used both fresh and dried.

8. Tamari and Nama Shoyu

These are special types of soy sauce that have not been pasteurized; made of fermented soybeans, wheat, sea salt and water. Tamari is wheat-free. They do not contain any preservatives.

9. Salt

I recommend using Celtic Sea Salt, a coarse sea salt with a grayish hue. Another delicious and nutritious salt is Himalayan pink salt, which you can find in health food stores.

10. Algae

Algae are an excellent protein source, and one of the best sources of iodine. You can find algae in many different food, medicinal, and cosmetic products. It has also been used throughout history for therapeutic purposes.

Spirulina—is a blue-green algae that is high in GLA (gamma-linolenic acid), which strengthens the blood vessels, balances blood pressure, reduces the risk of blood clots, and strengthens the body's immune system. Contains beta karotene, vitamin E, calcium, phosphorous, and magnesium. High in protein and makes a nutritionally rich addition to your diet. Keeps the skin healthy. You can find spirulina fresh or freeze-dried.

Arame—is an algae that is cut into small strips and should be soaked for five to ten minutes. Arame is good to begin with if you haven't eaten much algae before because it has a more mild ocean flavor compared to many other types of algae. Arame isn't as iodine-rich as other edible seaweeds, and it can therefore be eaten daily.

Ao nori—can be used like a spice; for example, you can sprinkle it on salads. It doesn't have a strong taste and is an easy way to get nutrients.

Not completely raw but okay!

There are certain products used in raw food cuisine that aren't completely raw but make the food taste so delicious that we use them anyway. Most often, they are used in very small quantities so that the dish is nevertheless 99% raw. Examples of these kinds of products include Dijon mustard, apple cider vinegar, balsamic vinegar, and pickled vegetables (which often contain sugar).

KITCHEN SUPPLIES

When I coach others, I arrive with my basket of produce in one hand and my food processor in the other. Other than a good knife and a cutting board, a food processor or a blender is the most important equipment for preparing raw food. A food processor is best for making mixtures such as dips and raw patés, and the blender works best for soups and drinks.

Knife—the type of knife one prefers can vary from person to person. Many people have a favorite knife that they use for everything. Sharpen the knife regularly; a sharp knife makes it more fun and easier to chop and cut.

Cutting board—some people recommend a glass cutting board that can easily be rinsed off. Plastic cutting boards also work; replace and recycle them somewhat regularly. I prefer a large wooden cutting board that I wash thoroughly after every use.

Cheese slicer—useful for slicing cucumbers, radishes, and carrots.

Peeler—you can make your own carrot and zucchini pasta.

Attractive bowls—when you are making food, it is easy to forget that presentation is just as important as taste. What is pleasing to the eye is pleasing to the palate.

Handheld blender—if you don't want to buy a full-sized blender, start by purchasing a good hand blender. You can also choose one that is sold together with a small food processor. Even if you want to upgrade your kitchen equipment later, you will always have a use for this.

Measuring cups—needed particularly at the beginning, until the eyes and the taste buds take over!

Fine-meshed strainer—for straining nut milks and rinsing sprouts.

Vegetable cleaning brush—in order to preserve as much of the root vegetables' nutrients as possible, keep the skin and only scrub away the dirt.

Grater—for grating food such as ginger, carrots, and apples.

2. taking the next step

TOWARD A RAW FOOD LIFESTYLE

At this stage, you have tried a variety of recipes and feel comfortable with the ingredients, and are interested in exploring further within the world of raw food. Maybe you are interested in experimenting more with sprouts and algae, and feel that it would be worth it to invest in new equipment and supplies to help simplify food preparation.

INGREDIENTS

Alfalfa sprouts—prove that it is possible for a tiny little seed to contain many important nutrients and protein! You should soak alfalfa seeds for four to six hours before you sprout them.

Mung bean sprouts—are rich in vitamins C and E. They sprout best in a plastic container; rinse twice a day, in the morning and the evening.

Whole wheat—when sprouted makes an excellent addition to both vegetable and fruit salads. You can also make bread from sprouted whole wheat.

Green lentils—taste sweet and mild. Easy to sprout and stores well in the refrigerator. Red lentils have already been heated and therefore cannot be sprouted.

Quinoa, red, black, and white—is a protein-rich grain that contains all of the eight essential amino acids. South American inhabitants have eaten quinoa since Incan times. Easy and quick to sprout. Try all the colors of quinoa as each has a distinctive flavor.

Wild rice—is the seed of a wild grass. Soak for approximately three days, and change the water every morning and evening. The rice is ready when it is al dente.

Prunes—are delicious, easy to find, and have a laxative effect.

Cranberries, dried or fresh—contain many antioxidants and are less sweet than many other fruits and berries.

Nori—are sheets of dried seaweed that are used in sushi. Buy the raw variety, even though these can be hard to find. You can also munch on these for a salty snack. Can be eaten daily.

Wakame—is an alga. Comes in flakes, pieces, or the entire sheet. Wakame has a salty taste which is reminiscent of a "fishy" flavor. If you eat wakame without soaking it first, remember that a tiny wakame flake will grow five times its original size when it is in your stomach.

Dulse—is a reddish-colored alga and a good source of protein, iron, and chlorophyll. A soft seaweed that comes from the British Isles. Limit your intake to once a week.

Wasabi powder—is made from horseradish and is often eaten with sushi.

Vanilla bean, whole pod or powder—makes a great addition to cashew cream or almond milk. Tastes delicious sprinkled over a fruit salad.

Sun-dried tomatoes—are available dried or soaked in oil. Sun-dried tomatoes soaked in oil contain a lot of fat, and the dried tomatoes need to be soaked for at least 20 minutes before being eaten. They can be hard to digest but are delicious.

KITCHEN SUPPLIES

Zester—a handheld grater that you can use to peel zest.

Lemon squeezer—for making your own citrus juices. A very good investment.

Chopsticks—eating with chopsticks makes you eat slower, which aids the digestive process.

Blender—used frequently in the raw food kitchen. When you work with dry ingredients, it is best to pulse the mixture and scrape the food from the sides of the blender intermittently.

Food processor—blends, mixes, chops, and purees your food. Simplifies food preparation.

Electric coffee mill—a simple, effective way to grind seeds and spices.

Sprouting containers—the easiest way to sprout at home.

Mortar and pestle—the traditional way to grind spices and seeds.

Salad spinner—dries rinsed salad greens. Another good trick is to put the greens in a kitchen towel and spin the towel around a few times (outside!).

Spiralizer/spiral slicer—you can use this to make squash and zucchini noodles, spaghetti from root vegetables, and decorative shapes from cucumber slices.

3. raw food enthusiast

The road from beginner to enthusiast isn't really that long. There are always new flavor combinations and kitchen gadgets to discover. Below are some ingredients and kitchen supplies that can be useful and fun to have if you want to eat entirely or almost completely raw. Some, but not all, of these ingredients and kitchen supplies are used in the recipes in this book.

INGREDIENTS

Raw cocoa—see carob/cocoa in the beginners ingredients list.

Maca powder—makes you strong, sexy, and strengthens the immune system. Made from the maca root, which grows in the Andes at 12,000 feet elevation.

Goji berries—contain all the essential amino acids as well as many antioxidants. A true superfood disguised as a little berry! Good in desserts. You can eat them as they are or blend them in a smoothie. Available in natural food stores.

Agave syrup/agave nectar—comes from a desert plant and has a low GI which makes it particularly good for people with diabetes. Tastes like honey.

Umeboshi plums—are pickled plums from Japan.

Mulberries—have a taste similar to that of toffee. Available in natural food stores.

Hemp seeds—are rich in protein and are scrumptious sprinkled over salads.

Green peas, whole wheat, un-hulled sunflower seeds, buckwheat, and hemp seeds, for sprouting—can be tricky to grow yourself but worth the time and effort if you have the space and the inclination. Miniature gardens promote health, happiness, and harmony.

Hijiki, kombu, kelp—are three more algae to introduce into your raw food lifestyle. Remember that it is best to only eat kombu once a month because it has a high concentration of iodine.

Fennel root—stabilizes blood sugar levels. Makes a good substitute for candy. Fennel seeds—can be eaten as after-dinner "mints" and are commonly done so in India. A good digestive aid and breath freshener. Makes an excellent substitute for gum.

Hemp oil, pumpkin seed oil, avocado oil, walnut oil, almond oil, coconut oil, saf-flower oil—are some suggestions for expanding your oil assortment. Try them out and see which ones you like the best. Don't forget that all your oil should be cold pressed and organic.

KITCHEN SUPPLIES

Dehydrator—a dehydrator is a tabletop oven that allows you to set the temperature to exactly 104 degrees. You can "cook" many dreamy delicacies, such as cakes, pizza and vegetable patties, and still have all the nutrients and enzymes present in the food. You can find dehydrators for $40 and up.

In order to make this book accessible for everyone, I haven't included any recipes that require a dehydrator. If you have an oven that can maintain a temperature around 104 degrees, you can use it instead of a dehydrator. However, conventional ovens often won't turn on at such low temperatures, and they don't work as well as a dehydrator. When using a conventional oven, you need to open the oven door periodically to release the air.

Juicer—this can be one of the more expensive investments you make for raw food preparation. A juicer allows you to make your own vegetable drinks and fruit juices. Try to find one that is easy to clean and that can handle larger chunks of food so you don't need to chop up the vegetables into small pieces before putting them in the juicer.

Gardening trays—if you want to sprout and convert your home into a beautiful mini greenhouse at the same time, these can be useful. Alternatively, you can use what you have—an old baking tray also works.

Nutcracker—you may already have this somewhere in your house. Nuts should ideally be bought with their shell on, in order to be 100% sure that they are fresh. But that requires more time than many of us have to spend on nuts!

Nut bag/cheesecloth—you can make your own seed "cheese" and "yogurt" by saving the leftover products when you make seed milk. But you need a bag or cloth. Can also work with a coffee filter if you don't make a large batch.

detoxing

WITH RAW FOODS WAS A NEW START!

Marie Andrén and seven of her coworkers detoxed for a week with raw food.

Marie Andrén's story: "This wasn't my first experience detoxing or eating raw food, and I was eager to try it again. When I had previously only eaten raw food for three days, I felt fantastic and I woke up early in the morning with tons of energy. When I heard of Erica's plan to bring raw food into the workplace, I knew I wanted to try it and I contacted her immediately. Eight of us at our workplace chose to participate in the raw food/detox week that Erica arranged."

First, we each had a one-on-one conversation with Erica where we discussed our reasons for detoxing while she explained what raw food is, and the reactions that can occur from a change in diet. Then we began. Erica came in the morning and brought food for breakfast, snacks, lunch and dinner. She often sat with us during lunch and told us about the food we had eaten or were going to eat that day. The vegetable and fruit salads were gorgeous and delicious! We ate lunch in the staff room, and many other employees became curious about what we were doing.

Before I went on the weeklong detox, I was going through a very stressful period in my work as manager of a spa. I felt tired and wasn't eating very well, and I had a hard time focusing. After only two or three days, my energy returned and I felt happier and more positive. Raw food doesn't only affect you physically, it also affects you mentally. It truly felt like a new start! As for side effects of the detox, someone in the group had a headache for part of the week, but I personally didn't have any trouble.

It was common practice for me to fast for ten days a year in order to cleanse my body, but I discovered that doing a raw food cleanse works better for me. During the fast I had a headache and felt like I had no strength, and it probably took me only a week after fasting to return to my old eating habits. But during a raw food diet, you have lots of energy and feel satisfied because you eat enough and you are aware of all the fantastic, delicious food that you are consuming. You don't feel hungry like you do both during and after a fast. Eating raw food for a week also caused me to eat less afterwards.

This is the third time that I have detoxed with raw and living foods, and it has showed me how good I can feel. I eat a blended, "regular" diet that consists of a little bit of fish and meat as well as lots of fresh vegetables (instead of potatoes, rice and bread). I buy more sprouts, beans, and fresh fruit. When I feel an urge to snack on something, I often eat nuts and seeds instead of bread and cake—they taste just as good anyway!

Marie Andrén, 46 years old, lives in Gothenburg, Sweden, and works as a spa manager and fitness consultant. Her biggest interests, both at work and on her own time, are "everything that has to do with wellness and health." She has two children, Olivia, 16 years old, and Benjamin, 14 years old.

Marie's detox advice: "Prepare yourself both physically and mentally before you begin detoxing. Get the facts about raw food, and then invest in it 100% to give yourself the chance for your body and soul to feel better."

Erica's advice:
Detoxing with raw food

I find that detoxing helps our bodies get rid of old waste products and fills us with new energy and vigor. Detoxing with raw foods provides our bodies with the proteins and antioxidants that they need. Raw food is food at its most nutrient-rich!

Certain symptoms are common during a detox, such as headache, fatigue, and loss of appetite. After detoxing, many people find it easier to distinguish between what the body actually needs and what we eat simply out of habit.

Try a three-day detox consisting of only raw food:

- Work your way into and out of the detox: eat vegan food (no animal products) two days before and two days after the detox.
- Eat three meals a day plus two snacks in between meals.
- It is often easiest to detox during the spring or summer.
- Make sure to drink enough water.
- Drink herbal teas that encourage the detoxification process. Ask the staff at a natural food store or a tea shop for more information.
- Rest when you are tired.
- Go on a walk, practice yoga, or do another form of gentle exercise.

breakfast

THE BEST WAY TO START YOUR DAY

It is called breakfast for a good reason, as we are literally breaking the fast from the night before. It is best to start your day with a glass of room temperature water with a slice of lemon. Then it's time for a fantastic breakfast!

Fruit Porridge with Celery

It sounds a little unusual to have celery for breakfast, but it gives the porridge a distinctive taste.

1 celery stalk (2 if you like the taste of celery), chopped into large
    pieces
1 kiwi, chopped into large pieces
1 small apple, chopped into large pieces
1 pear, chopped into large pieces
1 teaspoon cinnamon
1 tablespoon flaxseed, ground

1. Blend the celery and fruit in a blender, adding a little at a time.
2. Sprinkle the cinnamon and hulled flaxseed over the porridge.

TIP!
Buy the whole flaxseed and grind them yourself, with a coffee grinder, immediately before you plan to eat them. This way you get more of the healthy omega-3 fatty acids.

Store the ground flaxseed in a sealed jar in the refrigerator so they don't go bad.

Sweet Breakfast Porridge

A sweeter alternative to Fruit Porridge with Celery.
This is a filling and satisfying dish that won't leave a heavy feeling in your body.

1 banana, chopped into large pieces
1 apple, chopped into large pieces
1 pear, chopped into large pieces
1 teaspoon cinnamon
1 tablespoon flaxseed, ground

1. First put the pear into the blender; then add the banana and then the apple.
   Blending the fruit in this order prevents the mixture from getting too sticky.
2. Sprinkle the cinnamon and flaxseed over the mixture.

Granola

2 PORTIONS

¼ cup almonds, soaked
¼ cup sunflower seeds
¼ cup walnuts, soaked
4 fresh dates
¼ teaspoon cinnamon
Pinch of salt
1 fruit of choice, sliced
½–¾ cup almond milk (see the recipe on p. 137)

1. Put the nuts and sunflower seeds in the food processor and pulse until they are thickly cut.
2. Blend the dates, cinnamon, salt, and nuts together in a bowl.
3. Serve the granola with your choice of fruit and almond milk. Store in a sealed jar in the refrigerator. The granola will last for 2 days; it will last longer if you don't soak the nuts.

> **TIPS!**
> - Fresh apricots make a good addition to your granola breakfast.
> - You can create a delicious apple pie flavor by topping your granola off with sliced apple and a little bit of vanilla powder.

Muesli

1 PORTION (8 PORTIONS)

Buy the "raw" oats.

½ cup oats (4 cups)
2 tablespoons raisins (1 cup)
1 tablespoon almonds, chopped (½ cup)
1 tablespoon walnuts, chopped (½ cup)
2 teaspoons sunflower seeds (¼ cup)
2 teaspoons honey (¼ cup)

Serve with:
½–¾ cup almond milk
¼ cup blueberries or strawberries

1. Put the oats, raisins, almonds, walnuts, sunflower seeds, and honey in a bowl. Blend carefully with a spoon or fork.
2. Serve with almond milk and berries. If you make a bigger batch, wait to add the honey until right before eating. The muesli will keep in the refrigerator (in an airtight jar) for up to 3 months.

Buckwheat Porridge

This dish makes stomachs happy and healthy. Buckwheat is gluten-free and protein-filled. You can soak a large batch of buckwheat and store it in the refrigerator for several days. When buckwheat is sprouted it becomes even more nutritious. Don't forget to rinse it once a day.

½ cup buckwheat, soaked
1 date
1 apple, chopped into large pieces
Cinnamon, to taste

1. Soak the buckwheat overnight. You may have to rinse away the residue that has gathered.
2. Grind the buckwheat in a blender, adding water until you have a porridge-like consistency.
3. Add the date and then the apple to the mixture. Blend.
4. Add the cinnamon, and blend one last time.

Nut Porridge

A good start to the day, particularly during the winter months when we want a heavier breakfast.

½ cup almonds, soaked
¼ cup sesame seeds
¼ cup sunflower seeds
4 dates
Juice from 1 orange
1 tablespoon honey

1. Blend the nuts and seeds, adding the dates and orange juice as you pulse. Blend to porridge consistency.
2. Sweeten to taste with honey.

Berry Breakfast

Fresh berries are the best! This recipe also works with frozen berries, but let them thaw out before making this meal.

½ cup blueberries
½ cup raspberries
1 banana, sliced
1 inch piece of fresh ginger, grated
2 tablespoons hazelnuts, coarsely chopped
½ tablespoon cinnamon
Honey, to taste

1. Place the blueberries, raspberries, and banana in a bowl.
2. Grate the ginger over the fruit mixture.
3. Garnish with the hazelnuts and cinnamon, adding honey to taste.

Mango and Pineapple Smoothie

This drink is delicious, and it is especially good in the summer blended with ice. This drink is great for breakfast, as a snack or an after-dinner dessert.

TIP!

You can use frozen mango instead of ice.

¼ of a fresh pineapple, in chunks
1 small mango, chopped
Juice from 1 orange
Ice cubes (if desired)

1. If using ice, crush the cubes in a blender. Drop one ice cube at a time through the hole in the blender lid if you have never put ice in your blender before.
2. Place the thin ice shavings in a glass.
3. Blend the orange juice, pineapple, and mango. Pour the mixture over the ice.

Raspberry Greenery

Raspberries help to cover up spirulina's algae taste, and the combination creates a delicious and super-healthy drink. You can also experiment with the amount of spirulina powder you add. Three teaspoons of spirulina contains approximately 10 grams of protein.

Juice from 2 oranges
½ cup frozen raspberries
1 pear, chopped
1 teaspoon spirulina powder

Mix together all of the ingredients, except for the spirulina, in a blender. When the mixture has reached smoothie consistency, add the spirulina.

Grapefruit Juice with a Twist

Do you want to make grapefruit juice even healthier for you? Add fresh ginger and spirulina!

¼ of a fresh pineapple, in chunks
Juice from one grapefruit
Fresh grated ginger and spirulina, if desired

Blend in a blender. Serve it on ice if you want a refreshing summer drink.

Since childhood we have heard that we need a big breakfast in order to get us through the day. But a simpler, lighter breakfast consisting of fresh fruit and berries can help the body to relax and cleanse itself before we eat heavier food for lunch.

If you have a physically demanding job, exercise often, or simply feel as though you need something more substantial in the morning, add something filling in addition to fruit for breakfast. For example, you can have a glass of sesame seed milk, a sunflower seed sauce, or a handful of soaked almonds with your breakfast fruit salad.

You can also eat fresh fruit first, wait a while to see how it feels, and then eat a more filling snack one or two hours later. How does a fresh fruit breakfast work for you? Try it for a week or two and see!

Hawaiian Breakfast

Papaya skin should have a yellow-green color and yield to the gentle pressure of your thumb when the papaya is ripe. The inside should be salmon-colored. Papaya is a miracle worker for those of you who have problems with digestion, or if you suffer from an upset stomach. Papaya seeds also help with digestion. Buy the larger papayas, as there is a greater likelihood that they will become perfectly ripe.

½ papaya, peeled and sliced (remove the seeds)
1 passion fruit
Juice from 1 lime

1. Place the papaya slices on a platter.
2. Hollow out the passion fruit, and place on the platter.
3. Squeeze the lime juice over the fruit.

Fruit Salad

How many times have we passed up the same old fruit salad consisting of apples, pears, oranges, and bananas? Try a just as easy but much more exciting variation!

1 banana, sliced
1 nectarine, cut into wedges
1 bunch of purple grapes, halved
Strawberries, halved (fresh or thawed)

1. Mix the banana, grapes, and nectarine together in a bowl.
2. Garnish with strawberries.

Green Breakfast Juice

The stalks and leaves from carrots and beets are extremely nutritious and filled with chlorophyll, so don't forget about them when you make your juice! You can use fresh parsley instead of these stalks if you prefer. This recipe requires a juicer.

Fresh bunch of carrots
Stalk from a bunch of carrots (rinsed)
1 cucumber
2 inch piece of fresh ginger
1 lemon, peeled

Place all the ingredients in the juicer, adding the lemon last. Drink fresh!

snacks

ENERGY BOOSTERS!

Eating snacks as part of a raw food diet is just as important as eating meals. The point of snacking is to keep your energy levels up by maintaining a constant blood-sugar level, which allows us to have lots of energy through-out the day. These snacks also work well as breakfast or healthy desserts.

Raspberry Coconut Smoothie

This one is delicious and refreshing!

¼ cup raspberries, fresh or frozen
1 banana
1 cup apple juice
Fresh mint leaves
1 tablespoon coconut flakes

1. Blend the raspberries, banana, and apple juice in a blender.
2. Garnish with mint leaves and coconut flakes.

Green Energy Kick!

Drink this and feel your energy return.

1 handful of parsley
3 kiwis, chopped
½ inch fresh ginger, peeled and chopped
Water

1. Blend the parsley with a little water in a blender.
2. Add the kiwi and the ginger, and blend again.
3. Add a little water at a time until you achieve a smoothie consistency.

Buckwheat Yumminess

This is good comfort food! You can also try this recipe using other fruits.

½ cup buckwheat, soaked
1 persimmon, sliced
5 walnuts, chopped
3 dates, chopped
Cinnamon, to taste

1. Soak the buckwheat for approximately 8 hours, and rinse.
2. In a bowl, toss the buckwheat with the chopped walnuts, chopped dates, and sliced persimmon.
3. Add cinnamon, to taste.

Quick Sesame Treat

The mildly bitter taste of sesame seeds is offset nicely by the creamy avocado and honey.

½ cup sesame seeds
1 cup frozen strawberries, thawed
1 avocado, mashed
2 tablespoons macadamia nuts, chopped
1 tablespoon honey

1. Pulse the sesame seeds to a flour-like consistency in a blender.
2. Add the thawed strawberries and their juice.
3. Blend until you have a creamy consistency, adding water if necessary.
4. Put the mixture in a bowl. Add the mashed avocado to the mixture.
5. Garnish with the nuts, and add honey to taste.

These two recipes work best if you have soaked the dried fruit before, but if you've forgotten to do so, it also works with the un-soaked dried fruit and regular water.

Fig and Pear Compote

A quick and easy snack!

4 soaked figs, and the soaking water (about ½ cup)
1 large pear, cut into large pieces
½ inch fresh ginger, chopped
Cinnamon, to taste
Nutmeg, to taste

1. Soak the figs for several hours, or overnight.
2. Blend the pears, figs, and soaking water in a blender until consistency is similar to chunky applesauce.
3. Add ginger to the mixture. Blend.
4. Add cinnamon and nutmeg. Blend.

Apricot and Apple Soup

A delicious and snackalicious soup!

5 soaked apricots, and the soaking water (about ½ cup)
1 large or 2 small apples, cut into large pieces
Cinnamon, to taste

1. Soak the apricots for 8 hours, or overnight.
2. Blend the apricots with a little of the soaking water in a blender.
3. Add the apples and more water (if needed) to the mixture.
4. Add the cinnamon. Blend until desired consistency.

Sprouted Green Lentils with Apple

Many recipes are invented simply by using what's left in the kitchen. This is one of those recipes! This snack helps cure sweet cravings.

½ cup green lentils, sprouted (see sprouting section, p. 17)
1 apple (red or green), cubed
Cinnamon, to taste
Honey, to taste

1. Put the apple and the lentils in a bowl.
2. Add the cinnamon and mix the ingredients together by hand or with a spoon.
3. Add the honey.

Lettuce Sandwich

Eat either as a sandwich using the lettuce as bread, or eat with a spoon and use the lettuce as a plate. This can also be served as a side dish.

1 avocado
1 or 2 pears, chopped
Fresh coarsely chopped cilantro, to taste
1 large salad leaf of any variety

1. For a creamy consistency, blend the avocado and 1 pear in a blender. For a crunchier consistency, chop the second pear into small pieces and stir into the mixture.
2. Add the cilantro to taste.
3. Spoon the mixture onto a lettuce leaf.
4. Serve with salsa if desired (see recipe on p. 119).

Pomegranate Juice— Valentine's Day Drink

The pomegranate is very rich in antioxidants. Although typically a winter/spring fruit, pomegranates can be found year round. When a pomegranate is ripe, its seeds will be dark red. You need between 2 and 3 pomegranates (depending on the size and juiciness of each fruit) in order to make 1 glass of juice.

2 to 3 pomegranates

1. Juice the seeds in a food processor (you can save some to sprinkle on salads; they last for a day).
2. Strain the juice.
3. Serve in a wine glass.

TIP!
My mother-in-law from Egypt taught me this trick: cut the pomegranate in two and squeeze it to soften the skin. Hold the fruit over a container (seed side facing down) and then "hit" the seeds out with the back side of a spoon.

workout shakes

Almond Shake with Berries

This nutrient-rich drink makes for a satisfying snack. You can also substitute your favorite berries for the blueberries and strawberries.

1 cup almond milk (see basic recipes, p. 137)
1 or 2 fresh dates
¼ cup blueberries, fresh or frozen
¼ cup strawberries, fresh or frozen

1. Place the almond milk in the blender.
2. Sweeten by blending in one of the dates.
3. Add the berries, and blend again. If you want a sweeter taste, add the second date.

> **TIP!**
> Use frozen berries to make a raw "milkshake."

Banana and Carob Smoothie

This smoothie has lots of protein and calcium, thanks to the tahini.

1 cup water
1 tablespoon tahini (see basic recipes, p. 132)
3 dates
2 tablespoons honey
3 teaspoons carob
1 banana

1. Blend the water and the tahini in a blender.
2. Add the dates and/or the honey (depending on how sweet you want it), and add the carob.
3. Add the banana and blend. Add more carob if you want a stronger chocolate taste..

> **TIP!**
> Frozen bananas turn this smoothie into a "milkshake."

Fantastic After-Workout Smoothie

If you need some quick energy right after a workout, this drink is for you! This smoothie contains vitamin C, protein, fat, carbohydrates, plus all of the nutrients that spirulina has to offer. This drink also works well even if you haven't just exercised, but feel like you need something quick while you are waiting for dinner to be ready.

3 tablespoons sunflower seeds
Juice from 2 oranges
½ banana
1 teaspoon spirulina powder
1 teaspoon honey

1. Pulse the sunflower seeds to a flour-like consistency using a blender.
2. Add the orange juice and the banana, and blend.
3. Dilute the drink if necessary with a little water. Add the spirulina.
4. Sweeten with honey.

lunch

KEEP YOUR ENERGY LEVEL UP!

Lunch should ideally be satisfying but not include too much food; this helps maintain a constant blood sugar level throughout the day. A good salad, for example, is excellent for lunch. Chewing your food thoroughly will aid digestion. If we make it easier for our bodies to digest food, then we will have more energy to do other things. Digestion begins with chewing!

Yummy Pasta Leftovers

Pasta leftovers consist of the seedy cores of the zucchini. Even though you don't use these cores in making pasta noodles, don't throw them away! Instead, keep them in a plastic bag in the refrigerator and they will last for about two days. The leftovers will make a delicious salad ingredient. If you don't like celery, you can substitute radishes instead.

2 zucchini leftovers, cut into small pieces
½ yellow bell pepper, cut into small pieces
1 pear, cut into small pieces
1 celery stalk, thinly sliced
10 purple grapes, halved
½ cup white cabbage, cut into strips
1 avocado, cubed
¼ cup walnuts, halved

1. Mix the zucchini, pepper, pear, celery, and grapes together in a bowl.
2. Add the strips of cabbage.
3. Stir the cabbage and the avocado into the pasta salad.
4. Sprinkle with walnuts.

Yellow Squash Pasta with Olive Tapenade

If the squash pasta is too moist, layer the pasta strips in a colander, salting each layer. Let the pasta drain for about an hour. Yellow squash pasta has a nuttier taste than zucchini pasta.

1 yellow squash
2 carrots
Sun-dried tomatoes, to taste

Tapenade:
½ yellow or red bell pepper, chopped
½ cup pine nuts
Black olives, to taste
Lemon juice, to taste
Salt, to taste
Dried herbs, to taste

1. Using a potato peeler, peel the outer-most layer of the squash and carrots, and compost or discard the peelings.
2. Make the pasta by peeling the rest of the carrots and squash, excluding the seeds of the squash.
3. Mix together tapenade ingredients, and add to pasta. Add the sun-dried tomatoes.

Beet Soup

Who says that beet soup can only be borscht? Add a little apple and avocado and you have a sweeter taste, which balances out the earthy taste of the beet. The horseradish of course stays in the recipe, to give it that extra kick!

2 beets, chopped
1 apple, chopped
1 tablespoon lemon juice
1 avocado

Serve with:
¼ cup mung bean sprouts
½ avocado
1 inch horseradish, grated

1. Peel and chop the beets. Add one piece at a time to the blender.
2. Add the apple and a little water to the mixture. Blend.
3. Add the avocado and lemon juice. The more thorough the blending, the finer the beets, and the creamier the consistency will be. Choose how thick you would like your soup to be by adding water or not.
4. Serve with mung bean sprouts, sliced avocado, and freshly grated horseradish.

Celery Soup #1

2 PORTIONS

You can make endless variations of celery soup; experiment and find your favorite. This recipe makes a good base.

1 bunch of celery stalks, chopped
2 tomatoes, chopped
¼ cup fresh parsley
2 teaspoons lemon juice
2 teaspoons salsa (see recipe on p. 119) or dried chili peppers, to taste
1 avocado
Nama shoyu or tamari
½ cup water

Mix everything together in a blender or food processor, and add the nama shoyu or tamari to taste. Add more water for a thinner consistency.

Celery Soup, Asian Variation

A full-flavored celery soup.

½ bunch of celery stalks, chopped
¼ bell pepper (red, yellow, or green), chopped
½ avocado
2 teaspoons lemon juice
5–6 cherry tomatoes, or 1 large tomato
1 teaspoon nama shoyu
½ cup water
Pinch of cayenne pepper
Oregano, to taste

1. Blend all of the ingredients together in a blender and add the spices to taste. If you want a saltier taste, add a little more nama shoyu.
2. Add more water if you want a thinner consistency.

Avocado Soup

This soup will keep you full for a long time. Add a little more chili pepper or garlic for extra spice.

1 avocado
1 cup water
Red pepper flakes, or part of a
    dried chili pepper, cut into
    small pieces
1 garlic clove
Herb or sea salt, to taste
2 teaspoons lemon juice

Serve with:
¼ of a red onion, finely diced
1 tomato, cut into large pieces
¼ cup alfalfa sprouts

1. Mix all the soup ingredients together in a blender. Begin with the avocado and a little water, and then add the garlic, lemon juice, chili, and salt to taste.
2. Serve with red onion, tomato, and alfalfa sprouts.

Holiday Season Carrot Soup

This soup tastes like Christmas! Works well as an appetizer or a healthy dessert.

1 cup freshly squeezed orange juice
1 carrot, chopped
Pinch of salt
1 teaspoon honey
2 pinches of cardamom
5 cloves, ground
1 teaspoon cinnamon
Pinch of ginger
3 dates
¼ cup macadamia nuts, coarsely chopped

1. Put the orange juice and the carrot in a food processor. Blend until the carrots are finely chopped.
2. Add the spices and dates. Add honey for a sweeter taste. Blend until desired consistency. Sprinkle the macadamia nuts on top of the soup.

Carrot Soup with Fennel

1¼ cup freshly squeezed orange juice
1 carrot, chopped
2 inches fennel, chopped
¼ cup water
¼ inch fresh ginger
1 teaspoon vegetable broth, or to taste
2 dates
2 teaspoons dried, or 1 tablespoon fresh
   thyme

1. Put the juice, carrots and fennel into the food processor. Blend until the carrots and fennel are finely chopped.
2. Add the water, broth, dates, thyme, and ginger to taste. Blend to your liking.

Sam Aziz doing the yoga asana Vrksasana, or Tree Pose.

Yoga Salad with Pistachio Dressing

I make this salad before yoga class. This keeps my energy levels up, and it also makes it possible to do yoga right after lunch because your stomach isn't too full or heavy.

1 handful of arugula
1 handful of spinach
½ cup white cabbage, cut into
   strips
¼ yellow bell pepper, diced
½ cup sunflower sprouts
½ green apple, diced
¼ cup snow peas

Dressing:
¼ cup pistachios, soaked for about
   8 hours
½ avocado
½ yellow bell pepper
Nama shoyu or himalayan salt
1 tablespoon lemon juice
½–¾ cup water

1. Toss the salad ingredients together in a bowl.
2. To make the dressing, put the pistachios in a blender and blend until they are finely chopped.
3. Add the avocado and a little water, and keep blending.
4. Add the bell pepper, salt or nama shoyu, and lemon juice.
5. Add a little water at a time until it becomes a dressing-like consistency, and add extra lemon and nama shoyu or salt if desired.

◁ Fennel Salad

A beautiful, colorful salad with a distinctive taste.

½ of a fennel bulb, cut into small pieces
½ bunch of arugula
Seeds from ½ pomegranate
5 walnuts, coarsely chopped

1. Toss the fennel with the arugula and the pomegranate seeds.
2. Sprinkle the walnuts over the salad.

Maria's Student Salad

Try this salad when you have an empty refrigerator but still want something fresh. You can usually find a bag of carrots hidden somewhere in the back of your refrig-erator. My friend Maria ate this salad multiple times a week when she was a college student.

3 carrots, grated
3 tablespoons raisins
3 tablespoons sunflower seeds
Splash of lemon juice
1 tablespoon olive oil
Pinch of herb salt

1. Toss the carrots, raisins, and sunflower seeds together in a bowl.
2. Dress with olive oil, lemon juice, and salt.

Easy Lunch

A wonderfully easy and delicious lunch.

1 avocado
Alfalfa sprouts
Splash of lemon juice
Herb salt, to taste

1. Slice the avocado and place on a plate.
2. Garnish with alfalfa sprouts, lemon juice, and herb salt.

Raw Root Vegetable Salad

This is a twist on the traditional Swedish root vegetable salad.

1 piece celery root
1 small turnip
1 or 2 kohlrabi
3 carrots
1 green apple
2 inches of a leek, cut into thin strips
6 radishes, cut into thin strips
1 orange, in segments
½ package spinach
Fresh ginger, to taste
Mung bean sprouts

1. Coarsely grate the celery root, kohlrabi, turnip, carrots, and apple.
2. Place all of the ingredients in a bowl. Toss.
3. Grate a little extra ginger into the mix if you want to strengthen your immune system, or just enjoy the taste.
4. Garnish with mung bean sprouts.

Red and Green Wild Rice

2 PORTIONS

This dish tastes best with a green salad.

½ cup wild rice, soaked for 3 days
1 avocado, cubed
2 tomatoes, sliced
1 tablespoon olive oil
Juice from ¼ of a lemon
Salt, to taste

1. Soak the wild rice for 3 days; rinse and change the water every morning and evening.
2. Toss the wild rice, cubed avocado, and tomato slices together in a bowl.
3. Sprinkle olive oil and lemon juice over the mixture.
4. Toss again and salt if needed.

Waldorf Salad

The arame and clover sprouts bring out the taste of the other salad ingredients.

2 carrots, cut into rounds
1 celery stalk, thinly sliced
1 red apple, cut into small pieces
½ cup arame, soaked for 10 minutes
¼ cup raisins
3 tablespoons clover sprouts
Lemon juice, to taste
Olive oil, to taste
¼ cup walnuts, halved

1. Peel and cut the carrots.
2. Toss the celery, carrots, and apple with the arame, raisins, and sprouts in a salad bowl.
3. Sprinkle a little lemon juice and olive oil over the salad.
4. Garnish with walnuts.

1 Italian Salad

1 nectarine (or a peach), sliced
Red onion rings, about 10 or so
½ bunch of arugula
6 black olives (preferably Kalamata)
Olive oil, to taste
Lemon juice, to taste

1. Add the nectarine and red onion to the arugula.
2. Add the olives.
3. Sprinkle olive oil and lemon juice over the salad.

1

2 Greek Salad

1 red onion, cut into thin rings
1 green bell pepper, cut into thin rings
2 tomatoes, cut into rounds
½ cucumber, cut into rounds
Olive oil, to taste
Lemon juice, to taste
Herb blend (for example, dried thyme, oreg-ano, and rosemary), to taste
10 Kalamata olives

1. Toss all the vegetables in a salad bowl.
2. Squeeze the lemon juice on the salad, and add lots of olive oil.
3. Add the herbs.
4. Garnish with olives.

3 French Lunch Salad

¼ to ½ head romaine lettuce
6 radishes, cut into thin wedges
5 snow peas, cut into small pieces
1 carrot, cut into rounds
6 green olives
1 tablespoon capers

Serve with:
Quinoa sprouts

Dijon Vinaigrette:
¼ cup olive oil
¼ cup water
2 teaspoons dijon mustard

1. Rinse and tear or chop the romaine lett-uce into smaller pieces.
2. Add the radishes, snow peas, and carrots.
3. Add the olives and capers.
4. Dress the salad.
5. Serve with quinoa sprouts.

Kale Meets Mustard Seeds

There are black and yellow mustard seeds; the black seeds have a stronger taste. Kale and Brussels sprouts are common ingredients on our holiday dinner table. This is one of my favorite ways to prepare these nutrient-rich foods.

4 leaves of kale, cut into large pieces
½ tablespoon canola or flaxseed oil
Pinch of salt
2 teaspoons mustard seeds
5 to 8 Brussels sprouts, cut into small pieces
1 apple, cubed
3 tablespoons pecans, coarsely chopped

1. Grind the mustard seeds, using a blender, a mortar and pestle, or a knife. Dress the kale with the oil, salt, and mustard seeds.
2. Add the Brussels sprouts, apple pieces, and pecans. Toss.

Savoy Cabbage

2 PORTIONS

½ head of Savoy cabbage, cut into thin strips
1 bunch of mizuna salad
1 avocado, cubed
½ cup mung bean sprouts
Juice from 1 orange

Serve with:
½ cup arame, soaked for 10 minutes
Sauerkraut

1. Start by thoroughly rinsing the mizuna.
2. Add the Savoy cabbage, avocado, and mung bean sprouts.
3. Squeeze the orange juice over the salad.
4. Serve with arame and sauerkraut.

Purple Cabbage vs. Sprouters

A new twist on the old cabbage salad.

½ head of purple cabbage, cut into thin strips
3 tablespoons walnuts, coarsely chopped
1 orange, cut into small pieces
¼ cup alfalfa sprouts
1 handful sunflower sprouts

Toss the ingredients together.

> **TIP!**
> You can use a cheese slicer to make the cabbage strips.

Root Vegetable Noodles with Sauce

These healthy noodles and sauce may look a little boring, but the taste more than makes up for it.

Noodles:
1 small celery root
1 parsnip

Sauce:
2 Jerusalem artichokes
10 walnuts
1 tablespoon lemon juice
Horseradish, to taste
¼ cup water

1. Make root vegetable noodles with a spiralizer, zester, or grater.
2. Using a food processor, mix all of the sauce ingredients together.
3. Add horseradish if you want, and possibly a little more water, depending on desired consistency.
4. Put the noodles on a plate and pour the sauce over the noodles.

Sweet Potato Noodles with Jerusalem Artichoke Dressing

My foodie friend Martin fell in love with this dish, and this was the first time he tried raw foods! Jerusalem artichokes have a nutty, mild flavor, and they taste just as good raw or cooked. Also, making noodles and pasta is a good way to eat root vegetables, and it makes for cheap eating!

1 sweet potato

Dressing:
1 tablespoon water
1 Jerusalem artichoke
¼ cup walnuts
2 tablespoons raisins
½ yellow or red bell pepper
2 teaspoons lemon juice
Pinch of salt
Chili flakes, to taste

TIP!
If you don't have a spiralizer or zester, use a grater instead.

1. Make sweet potato noodles with a spiralizer or a zester.
2. Put the Jerusalem artichoke in the food processor, and blend.
3. Add the water, walnuts, raisins, and pepper. Pulse until smooth.
4. Add lemon juice, salt and possibly more water to taste.
5. Pour the dressing over the noodles.
6. Garnish with chili flakes if you want a little spice.

Matthew Griffiths, 34 years old, is an educator and personal trainer. He has his own business and is also a firm believer in raw food: "This food gives strength, energy, and vitality!" He is originally from London but currently lives in Gothenburg, Sweden with his wife Malin and their children, 5-year-old Olivia and 18-month-old Charlie. "Our kids eat quite a bit of raw food. They really like homemade juices and frozen berry 'ice cream.'" He enjoys spending his free time with those he loves.

Matthew's raw food tip: "Buy a juicer and make your own energy drinks."

Matthew Griffiths has always been interested in diet and health:
I was immediately a fan of raw food because I like its natural simplicity, and it gives me lots of energy. The food I eat has to be high in nutritional content and have a cleansing effect, in order to help me feel and look good.

Matthew wakes up early in the morning, either for his own workout or to meet his customers who want to visit the gym before work.
This is what an average day looks like for me: breakfast consists of homemade juice if I start working at six am. When I start work even earlier, I eat a more substantial breakfast typically consisting of fruit porridge with nuts and seeds. For snacks throughout the day, I eat nuts, dried fruit, and grains, and I drink vegetable or fruit juices. At least half of my lunch and dinner usually consists of raw food.

Matthew trains quite a bit, typically six to eight hours a week. Before a marathon or bike race, he often trains between 12 and 16 hours a week.
Immediately before and after working out, I have a flaxseed smoothie or dried fruit and nuts. My intake of protein depends on my type of workout and its length and intensity. I am not a vegetarian, so the majority of my protein intake comes from fish and meat. I plan to increase my intake of nuts, seeds and sprouts.

Eating a high quantity of raw food gives me a more consistent energy level throughout the day. My body assimilates raw food quickly, especially when I am working out a lot. This means that when I eat raw food, I can eat more often and still feel energetic and light in my body.

The majority of people Matthew meets react positively and become curious when they notice how much raw food he eats.

Everyone has heard of the negative effects of eating food that contains additives and chemicals. Eating raw food automatically decreases your chances of consuming chemicals and additives because it is made from all-natural ingredients. Plus very few people understand just how versatile raw food can be, and how many delicious flavors can be created from it!

EATING LOTS OF

raw food

GIVES ME A CONSISTENT ENERGY LEVEL THROUGHOUT THE DAY.

Matthew Griffiths, 34 years old, educator and personal trainer, has always been interested in diet and health.

dinner

I'M HUNGRY AND I WANT TO EAT NOW!

A weekday dinner should have a short preparation time and be easy to make, but at the same time be delicious and nutritious. Weekends and holidays are typically more convenient times to experiment with new foods, and to spend more time buying ingredients and preparing a more extensive dinner.

Broccoli Salad with Raisins

2 PORTIONS

Proof that dinner doesn't have to be complicated to be a success!

1 large crown of broccoli, cut into bite-sized pieces
1 teaspoon salt
1 tablespoon olive oil
3 carrots, coarsely grated
1 red onion, finely diced
1 tomato, chopped
5 sun-dried tomatoes, cut into small pieces
1 apple, cubed
¼ cup raisins
¼ cup sunflower seeds
1 tablespoon lemon juice

1. Coat the broccoli with salt and olive oil, to soften it.
2. Add the other fruits and vegetables to the broccoli.
3. Sprinkle the raisins and sunflower seeds on the salad.
4. Dress with lemon juice, and toss thoroughly.

TIP!

Do you want to invite your friends or family over to a raw food dinner? Here is my advice for a three-course meal that could convince even the biggest skeptic!

* Beet Soup, p. 66.
* Raw Lasagna, p. 107.
* Fluffy Chocolate Mousse with Cheesecake, p. 152 and 163

Indian Cauliflower Mash

This recipe is also listed under basic recipes. Here is an Indian variation.

1 head of cauliflower
1 cup cashew nuts
1 tablespoon olive oil
½–1 teaspoon salt
Spices: garam masala or curry and paprika, to taste
Fresh cilantro or parsley, to taste

1. Cut the cauliflower into small pieces and put into a food processor. Pulse until finely chopped.
2. Remove the cauliflower, and put the cashews into the food processor. Pulse until finely chopped.
3. Now add the cauliflower in together with the cashews and continue to blend.
4. Add oil and salt, and blend until smooth.
5. Season with the spices.
6. Remove the mash from the food processor, and garnish with cilantro or parsley.

Spinach and Cashews

A refreshing salad. The mild taste of
the cashews works nicely in combination with the salty sun-dried tomatoes.

½ *package fresh spinach*
1 *tomato, cut into large pieces*
½ *bell pepper (any color), cut into large*
    pieces
2 *sun-dried tomatoes, cut into thin strips*
4 *large mushrooms, thinly sliced*
5 *to 8 basil leaves*
Pinch of salt
1 *tablespoon lemon juice*
6 *cashew nuts*

1. Toss the tomato, pepper, sun-dried
   tomatoes, and mushrooms together
   with the spinach.
2. Add the basil.
3. Pour the lemon juice over the salad.
   Toss.
4. Sprinkle the cashew nuts (break
   them into smaller pieces first using
   your hand) and salt over the salad.

Spinach and Arugula Salad

A green and clean walnut salad!

½ package spinach
½ of a bunch of arugula
1 celery stalk, cut into rounds
1 green apple, cubed
4 radishes, chopped
2 inches of cucumber, sliced
1 avocado, cubed
6 walnuts, coarsely chopped
Juice from ½ of a lemon
1 tablespoon honey

1. Mix the spinach and arugula together in a bowl.
2. Add the celery, apple, radish, cucumber, and avocado pieces.
3. Add the walnuts and lemon juice. Toss.
4. Sprinkle honey over the salad.

TIP!
To make your honey runnier, add a little lukewarm water.

Friday Burritos

2 PORTIONS

Who says that a burrito has to involve a tortilla?! A romaine lettuce "tortilla" makes for a crispier and healthier meal.

Several romaine leaves

Burrito Filling:
1 avocado, mashed
3 radishes, finely chopped
½ yellow bell pepper, finely chopped
1 tomato, finely chopped
2 sun-dried tomatoes, finely chopped
1 inch of a leek, finely chopped
1 sprig of parsley, finely chopped
1 teaspoon tamari
Pinch of dried chili flakes
Juice from ½ of a lime
2 tablespoons sunflower seeds
½ cup alfalfa sprouts

1. Stir the radishes, pepper, tomato, sun-dried tomatoes, leek, and parsley into the mashed avocado.
2. Season with the tamari, lime juice, and chili flakes.
3. Rinse and dry the romaine leaves.
4. Put a large spoonful of the mixture onto each leaf.
5. Add sunflower seeds and alfalfa sprouts to the avocado mixture.
6. Roll the romaine leaves into a burrito.

Wakame Burritos

2 PORTIONS

Wakame tastes like the ocean. When you are spicing up your burritos with wakame, remember that it swells to about 5 times its original size in your stomach.

Several romaine leaves

Burrito Filling:
1 avocado, mashed
8 cocktail tomatoes, finely chopped
1 garlic clove, finely chopped
Corn kernels from 1 ear
1 sprig of fresh basil, coarsely chopped
Tamari, to taste
Salt, to taste
Pinch sambal oelek (use a little bit of a red chili pepper if you don't have this spice)
1 tablespoon wakame

1. Add the tomato and garlic to the avocado mash.
2. Stir in the corn.
3. Season with the basil, tamari, salt, and sambal oelek.
4. Put a large spoonful of the mixture onto each leaf.
5. Garnish with wakame before rolling your burritos.

Weekend Taco Special

Celebrate the weekend with a healthier twist on traditional tacos. Use the lettuce leaves as your taco shell, add the filling below, and choose any additional fillings you want. Serve your tacos with tomato wedges and marinara sauce (see p. 107), and with sour cream cheese (see p. 140).

Lettuce leaves

Filling:
½ cup pistachios, soaked
½ cup walnuts, soaked
1 carrot, chopped
3 inches of a leek
2 teaspoons nama shoyu
Taco spices

Choose Your Additional Fillings:
tomatoes, corn, pepper, cucumber, celery, yellow onion, jalapeños, salsa

1. Soak the nuts for 8 hours.
2. Pulse the nuts in a food processor until they are coarsely chopped.
3. Take out the nuts. Put the carrots, leeks, and nama shoyu in the food processor, and pulse until vegetables are finely chopped.
4. Toss the nuts and vegetables together in a bowl. Season with the spices.

Stuffed Peppers

6 PORTIONS

A popular dish among my dinner guests.

1 cup walnuts, soaked, finely chopped
1 cup hazelnuts, soaked, finely chopped
3 small carrots, finely chopped
5 inches of a leek, finely chopped
2 teaspoons tamari
3 bell peppers of any color
Arugula and sunflower sprouts, for garnishing

1. Soak the nuts for approximately 8 hours, or overnight.
2. Finely chop the nuts, carrot, and leek one ingredient at a time, using a food processor.
3. Mix all the ingredients together in a bowl, and add the tamari.
4. Seed and cut the peppers in half, and fill the peppers with the mixture.
5. Place the arugula leaves on a serving platter, and arrange the peppers on top of the leaves. Garnish the peppers with sunflower sprouts. You can store any extra pepper filling in the fridge, as it lasts for up to 2 days (freezing also works).

Parsley Tabbouleh

6 PORTIONS

An almond-filled variation of North African tabbouleh.

4 handfuls of curly parsley, finely chopped
4 handfuls of flat parsley, finely chopped
6 tomatoes, cut into small cubes
1 ½ avocados, cut into small cubes
2 small red onions, finely chopped
½ cup almonds, pre-blended to a flour-like consistency

1. Rinse the parsley thoroughly.
2. Mix all ingredients together in a bowl.
3. Make the dressing, and pour the dressing over the tabbouleh. Let the dressing sink in for a few minutes before eating.

Dressing:
Juice from 1 lemon
¼ cup olive oil
Pinch of salt

Beet Burgers on Romaine Buns

2 PORTIONS

Raw beets can provide a surprising variety of tastes.
See if this one surprises you.

3 beets
2 carrots
¼ cup pistachios, optional
½–1 avocado
2 teaspoons lemon juice
Pinch of sea salt
1 or 2 teaspoons Dijon mustard
Several romaine lettuce leaves
Capers to taste, for garnishing

1. Finely chop/grate the beets and the carrots, either using a food processor or a grater.
2. Put the beets, carrots, and pistachios into the food processor.
3. Add the avocado, and blend.
4. Season with lemon juice, sea salt, and mustard. Start with one teaspoon of mustard, adding a little more if you want a stronger taste.
5. Put about ½ cup of the mixture on each romaine leaf; garnish with capers.

Papaya Carpaccio

2 PORTIONS

A ripe papaya skin yields to the touch, and its insides are salmon-colored. This dish works well with the hot salsa (see recipe p. 119). Take away the spinach and dates, and you've got an excellent appetizer.

1 papaya, sliced
1 package baby spinach
Juice from 1 lime
¼ cup pecans, coarsely chopped
4 dates, cut into small pieces
1 or 2 tablespoons olive oil, if desired

1. Halve and seed the papaya.
2. Cut the papaya into thin pieces.
3. Place the spinach onto a plate, and arrange the papaya on the spinach.
4. Squeeze the lime onto the papaya and spinach.
5. Sprinkle the pecans and the dates over the papaya.
6. Add olive oil, if desired.

Sushi

2 PORTIONS

When I introduce raw food sushi at presentations, I inevitably hear "but sushi is already raw." True, the fish and vegetables are often raw, but the rice is cooked, the soy sauce processed, and the nori is roasted. Raw food sushi consists of unroasted nori (this can be hard to find), tamari, and raw fillings and spices that make it taste like the real thing.

Suggested Sushi Fillings:

- *Soak 1 cup of pine nuts for 2–4 hours. Blend in a blender with a little water, and add wasabi powder until the spice is just right for your taste buds.*
- *Blend ½ cup of almonds to a flour-like consistency using a blender. Add a little olive oil, salt, paprika, curry, and turmeric, and blend again.*
- *Avocado slices, finely chopped leek, a little grated horseradish and chopped Brazil nuts. This roll tends to be the most popular, so make twice as much as you think you'll need!*

Serve with nori, tamari, and pickled ginger. For a fishier taste, sprinkle wakame flakes on the filling. More filling suggestions include combinations of sliced carrot, cucumber, radishes, tomatoes, sprouts, celery, leeks, and pepper. To roll sushi, put the nori flat on a clean surface and place the filling ingredients in the middle of the nori. Carefully pull the ingredients tightly together while rolling the nori into a roll.

Raw Lasagna

Someone once told me that this dish is "manly," and by that they meant that it's often well-received by skeptical, meat-eating males!

TIP!

Flaxseed crackers, sour cream cheese, and arugula work well with this dish.

5 mushrooms of your choice, thinly sliced
1 tablespoon olive oil
½ tablespoon tamari
2 zucchini, peeled
½ package spinach
6 tablespoons (about ½ cup) marinara sauce (recipe below)
1 or 2 avocados, sliced

1. Marinate the mushrooms in olive oil and tamari for 10 minutes. Remove the excess liquid with a paper towel.
2. Thinly slice the zucchini, making long noodle shapes using a potato peeler or a knife.
3. Put the spinach and a little water in a food processor, and pulse until it becomes a sauce. Put the sauce in a bowl.
4. Cover the bottom of a rectangular baking dish with 2 tablespoons marinara sauce, and put about a third of the zucchini slices on top of the sauce.
5. Add 2 tablespoons of the marinara sauce and half of the mushrooms, gently pressing the ingredients down as you go.
6. Add a third of the zucchini again, half of the avocado slices, and half of the spinach sauce.
7. Add the last third of the zucchini, and 2 tablespoons of the marinara sauce. Add the rest of the spinach sauce and avocado. Put the last layer of mushrooms on the top of the lasagna.

Marinara Sauce

You can use this as a lasagna sauce, zucchini pasta sauce, or as its own side dish.

2 tomatoes
5–6 sun-dried tomatoes
½ red bell pepper
2 teaspoons olive oil

1 tablespoon fresh basil, or 1 teaspoon
    dried basil
1 teaspoon dried oregano
Salt, garlic, cayenne pepper to taste

Put all the ingredients in a food processor and blend. This sauce lasts for 3 days in the fridge.

I Can't Believe It's Not Salmon Paté

The color and spices in this dish remind me of salmon paté.

¾ cup sunflower seeds, soaked
¾ cup almonds, soaked
2 tablespoons water
1 carrot, chopped
1 scallion, finely chopped
½ sprig of dill, chopped
Pinch of salt
1 tablespoon lemon juice

Garnish with:
1 lemon, sliced
Sprig of dill

Serve with:
Salad greens

1. Soak the almonds and sunflower seeds for 4 to 8 hours.
2. Put all of the ingredients into a food processor. Process to a smooth consistency. Season with extra salt, lemon juice, and dill, if desired.
3. Form the mixture into a paté on a serving dish.
4. Garnish with dill and lemon slices.

Asian Cashew Curry

A crispy salad accompanied by a delicious cashew curry dressing.

Salad:
½ head of crispy lettuce, torn or chopped
   into bite-sited pieces
½ cup wild rice, soaked
1 green apple, cubed
2 inches of a leek, cut into rounds
¼ small head of cabbage, cut into thin
   strips
2 celery stalks, cut into rounds
¼ head of cauliflower, cut into bite-sized
   pieces

1. Soak the wild rice for 3 days.
2. Rinse every morning and evening,
   and change the water once a day.
3. Toss the rice with the other ingredients in a bowl.
4. Serve with cashew curry dressing.

Cashew Curry Dressing:
½ cup cashew nuts
½ cup water
¼ yellow bell pepper
1 inch of a leek
Curry, turmeric, tamari, and lemon juice, to
   taste

1. Blend the nuts into a flour-like consistency using a blender.
2. Add the pepper and the leek, and
   half of the water.
3. Blend until thoroughly mixed.
4. Add a little water at a time until the
   dressing reaches a creamy consistency.
5. Season with the spices, tamari, and
   lemon juice.

My Brother's Banana Curry

My brother wants the same thing every
year for his birthday; here is a raw variation.

1 banana, sliced
¼ cup coconut flakes
¼ cup raisins
1 mandarin orange, in segments
¼ cup peanuts, coarsely chopped
½ cup wild rice, soaked (see numbers 1 and
   2 above)

Serve with:
Cashew curry dressing

> **TIP!**
>
> You can either place all the ingredients to-
> gether in one bowl and serve with the dress-
> ing already tossed, or you can put the ingre-
> dients into separate bowls and have everyone
> serve themselves.

Parsnip Couscous

2 PORTIONS

Parsnip, when pulsed in the food processor, has the same consistency and taste as couscous. A great way to add a little extra oomph to your salad.

1 parsnip, chopped
1 celery stalk, cut into small pieces
¼ cucumber, cut into rounds
   and quartered
2 pears, cut into small pieces
2 large portions of crispy salad
   greens of choice
1 avocado, cubed

Dressing:
1 teaspoon honey
2 tablespoons olive oil
2 tablespoons lemon juice
Pinch of salt

Garnish with:
3 tablespoons walnuts, coarsely
   chopped

1. Put the parsnip into a food processor and pulse until it becomes grainy.
2. Combine the dressing ingredients to make the dressing.
3. Toss the other salad ingredients together with the dressing, and serve on a plate.
4. Place the parsnip couscous on top of the salad.
5. Garnish with walnuts.

Going Nuts for Pink Pepper

I dreamt up this dish because I was missing the days when I ate chicken with soy sauce and pink pepper. I created the raw version, and it tasted just like I remembered, except even better! The Brazil nuts add a refreshingly crunchy texture.

1 handful of celery root, chopped
4 Jerusalem artichokes, chopped

Brazil Nut Dressing:
½ cup Brazil nuts, soaked
1 tablespoon water
1 teaspoon honey
1 teaspoon lemon juice
Pinch of salt
1 teaspoon tamari
3 teaspoons pink pepper

Serve with:
Arugula

1. Soak the Brazil nuts for 8 hours.
2. Chop the nuts in a food processor.
3. Add half of the water, and the honey, lemon, salt, tamari, and pink pepper to the food processor. Blend until smooth, adding more water if needed.
4. Set aside the dressing.
5. Process the celery root and the artichokes until they become "rice" in the food processor.
6. Serve the Brazil nut dressing and vegetable rice together with the arugula.

side dishes

DELICIOUS!

Side dishes are great to have ready-made in the refrigerator, to be eaten by themselves or as part of a larger meal.

Flaxseed Crackers

1½ cups flaxseed
¼ cup sesame seeds
¼ cup pumpkin seeds
¼ cup sunflower seeds
½ cup water
1 teaspoon spice/spices of your choice (I recommend cumin)
1 teaspoon salt

TIP!
Soak the flaxseed for 2 to 4 hours before baking.

1. In a large mixing bowl, add the flaxseed, sesame seeds, pumpkin seeds, and sunflower seeds to the water. Add more water if needed to achieve a consistency like that of oatmeal.
2. Add the spices and salt. Thoroughly mix by hand.
3. Spread out a thin layer of the mixture onto a baking sheet and put in a dehydrator or the oven, set to between 100 and 115 degrees. Open the oven door periodically to release some of the heat. It takes between 8 and 24 hours to bake these, depending on the type of oven.
4. When the crackers are crispy and easy to break into pieces, they are done. Store in a well-sealed container.

See page 140 for the sour cream cheese recipe.

Golden Flaxseed Crackers

This is a sweeter version of the above recipe. Golden flax has a fuller taste than the brown flaxseed, and the golden flax gives a richer color.

1 ½ cups golden flaxseed
1 cup water
2 tablespoons honey
2 teaspoons cinnamon

1. In a large mixing bowl, mix the flaxseed and water until you achieve a thick consistency. Start with ¼ cup of water and add a little at a time if needed. Let the mixture rest for a few hours.
2. Add a little more water if the mixture has thickened so much that you can't move it.
3. Add the honey and the cinnamon. Mix well.
4. Spread out a thin layer of the mixture onto a baking sheet and put it in a dehydrator or the oven, set to between 100 and 115 degrees. Open the oven door periodically to release some of the heat. It takes between 8 and 24 hours to bake these, depending on the type of oven.
5. Serve with coconut fat or oil as a substitute for butter. Store in a well-sealed container.

Avocado Lemongrass Dip

A guacamole variation, good as a side dish, but equally yummy as a dip for carrots, cucumber slices, and celery sticks.

1 avocado
1 lemon grass stalk
¼ red chili pepper
Pinch of chili flakes
2 apricots, soaked
1 or 2 tablespoons of the soaking water from the apricots
1 teaspoon tamari

1. Put all of the ingredients in a food processor. Start by adding a little bit of the chili pepper if you don't want too much spice.
2. Remove any remaining large pieces that have not mixed in well.

Hot Salsa

Experiment with this recipe. For example, try using a scallion instead of a red onion, try different chili pepper varieties, and see if you prefer lemon or lime juice. The super strong habanero pepper will really clear out your sinuses—even while you are chopping it! I recommend using plastic gloves while chopping peppers, or washing your hands immediately afterwards.

2 green chili peppers
2 red chili peppers
4 cloves garlic
1 red onion
½ cup olive oil
¼ cup lemon juice or lime juice
Pinch of salt

1. Seed the chili peppers and peel the garlic, discarding the seeds and peel.
2. Finely chop all of the ingredients, and blend them with the lemon or lime juice and the olive oil. This recipe gives an extra kick to many different dishes. Lasts for about 2 weeks in a glass jar in the refrigerator.

1 French Guacamole

French-inspired guacamole.

1 avocado
2 sun-dried tomatoes, cut into small pieces
3 chives
1 teaspoon Dijon mustard

1. Put all the ingredients in the food processor, and pulse until mixture is smooth.
2. Add more mustard if you want a stronger taste.

2 Pumpkin Parmesan

This makes a great topping to lots of dishes, especially zucchini pasta!

½ cup pumpkin seeds
½ teaspoon salt

Pulse the pumpkin seeds to a flour-like consistency using a blender, and add the salt.

2

1

Pine Nut and Basil Pesto

Cheese is a common ingredient in traditional pesto, but with these raw ingredients, you won't miss that cheese! Raw pesto, *prego!*

½ cup pine nuts
½ cup olive oil
1 sprig of basil
2 teaspoons sea salt
Lemon juice, to taste

1. Blend the pine nuts in a blender.
2. Add the olive oil and pulse carefully in the blender, while periodically scraping the mixture from the sides.
3. Add the basil leaves and pulse.
4. Season with sea salt and a little lemon juice. Lasts for a week in the refrigerator.

Tapenade

This tastes so much better than the store-bought variety.

½ cup black olives
¼ cup olive oil
3 garlic cloves, finely chopped
3 teaspoons capers

1. Remove the olive pits.
2. Blend the olives in a blender until they are finely chopped.
3. Add the oil, garlic, and capers, and blend. Lasts for 2 weeks when refrigerated.

3

4

5

Green Olive Tapenade

A simple and delicious tapenade.

½ cup green olives
¼ cup olive oil
3 garlic cloves, finely chopped

1. Pit the olives. Blend in a blender until finely chopped.
2. Add the oil and finely chopped garlic, and blend. Lasts for 2 weeks in the fridge.

Marinated Carrots, Broccoli, Cauliflower, and Leek

Vegetables marinated in olive oil, salt, and lemon are perfect al dente—they are just the right texture and taste. Marinating vegetables makes their "raw" taste and texture disappear.

1. Cut the broccoli and cauliflower into bite-sized pieces. Cut the carrots and leek into thick strips.
2. Put the broccoli and cauliflower into a bag, and put the carrots and leak into another bag.
3. Add lots of olive oil and lemon to each bag, and add a good amount of salt.
4. Seal each bag, and put each bag in another bag to avoid any olive oil explosions.
5. Press the bag together so the olive oil and lemon really soak into the vegetables.
6. Place the bags in the refrigerator for about 8 hours. You can serve immediately, but the taste is stronger if you let the vegetables marinate for a few hours.

Do you want to marinate with tamari, and fresh and/or dried spices? Go for it! Experiment until you've found your favorite; I recommend oregano, basil, and thyme.

Herb-marinated Mushrooms and Onions

Marinated mushrooms have a taste very similar to fried mushrooms.

10 portobello mushrooms or other mushrooms, thinly sliced
Red onion, thinly sliced

Marinade:
Herb spices (for example thyme, rosemary, basil), to taste
1 teaspoon salt
¼ cup olive oil
Splash of lemon

1. Put the ingredients in the marinade.
2. Marinate for 30 minutes, turning over the mushrooms and onion after 15 minutes. Remove from the marinade, taking away any excess liquid with a paper towel.
3. Arrange the vegetables on a platter, and serve.

Kevin's Mustard

Kevin taught me how to make homemade raw mustard. Thanks, Kevin—this recipe is delicious!

½ cup mustard seeds, yellow or brown, soaked overnight
1 tablespoon salt
2 tablespoons apple cider vinegar
½ cup of vinegar-free pickle juice or sauerkraut juice
1 teaspoon turmeric

1. Soak the mustard seeds overnight, 1 part mustard seeds to 4 parts water. Drain off soaking water.
2. Blend the seeds with the apple cider vinegar, salt and pickle juice (or sauerkraut juice) in a blender. Put the mixture in a glass jar, add the turmeric, and stir all the ingredients together.
3. Put the lid on the jar, and shake it. Let the mustard "yeast" at room temperature for 2 days, preferably in a sunny windowsill. Lasts for 1 month in the refrigerator.

For 3½ years, 66-year-old Bitte Palmcrantz has been a high raw–vegan, which means that raw food makes up 85–90 percent of her diet. She likes to be out in nature and physically active, meet friends, play with her grandkids, read, and be politically active.

Bitte's raw food tip: "If you are an active person, it is often best to take it one step at a time. Start by eating a raw breakfast, and after a while, add more raw food to your diet."

BEST OF ALL IS THE EXTRA

energy

THAT I GET FROM EATING RAW FOOD.

One person who felt inspired to eat a raw food diet is Bitte Palmcrantz, Erica's mother.

Bitte Palmcrantz:

Erica was literally shining when she came home from the States, and had eaten only raw food for two months. Her skin looked gorgeous. I remember noticing such a big change that I thought: "What is going on here?!" I immediately became curious and interested.

A few months before going raw, Bitte Palmcrantz had already started to make changes in her diet. She stopped eating, among other things, sugar and white flour.

I had already prepared myself in some ways to go raw!

At the time, Bitte worked as a teacher for refugee children. After the school year had ended, she decided to start eating only raw foods.

I wanted to feel how eating raw food affected me, so I immediately started eating exclusively raw.

With Erica's help and help from a book about living food (a diet that is very similar to raw food), the transition to eating only raw food went surprisingly smoothly, Bitte says.

I went through my refrigerator and said to myself, "I can't have this! And I can't have this anymore either!" I gave all of the food to my son, and then I went out and bought the food that I needed to make the recipes in the living food book. The book said that I should sprout everything myself, but I decided to make it easier for myself, so I bought the sprouts instead.

It wasn't only her summer vacation and positive attitude that made it easier to transition to a raw food diet, it was also the fact that she lived alone.

If I had a husband at home who loved meat it would have been a whole lot harder. But living alone allows me to be egocentric and think only about myself!

Because of the significant change in her diet, Bitte had prepared herself for some kind of physical reaction, but nothing overly dramatic happened.

The first three or four days my stomach was a little upset.

One less positive aspect of raw food is all the cutting and chopping in the kitchen, an activity that Bitte has never been particularly fond of. But she says that she has learned to live with it:

And with this food I don't have any extra cooking time.

Bitte noticed almost immediately that she felt very healthy while eating raw food, and this is why she has stuck with it, even thought it can be a challenge to combine diet with social life.

In the beginning, I was almost fanatical. For example, when I was invited to someone else's house, I brought my own food with me. As a consequence, I had to answer so many questions all the time about my diet, and I felt like that was all I was talking about to my friends and acquaintances. Even though regular vegetarian food is no longer thought of as strange, this type of diet is considered very unusual, and many people want an explanation.

After several months of eating raw food, Bitte felt that she had become boring, as her diet distanced her from her social life and friends. She decided to compromise.

Today I eat about 85 to 90 percent raw food. I eat cooked and fried vegetarian food when I am out with friends, but when I am in my own home and in my own routines, I eat almost entirely raw. Sometimes I "cheat" by eating a whole wheat sandwich with a little cheese; I don't eat this every day, but every once in a while when I feel like it. For a luxurious treat, I buy a little extra dark chocolate!

Bitte often plans her meals several days in advance, which makes it easier to fit soaking and sprouting into her daily routine.

I am used to planning my meals in advance. I live out in the countryside, so I can't just walk to the store if I forget something.

Bitte was healthy and happy before beginning with raw food, even though she was a little overweight (she weighed 185 lbs and is 5'8"), and had to take medicine for high cholesterol. After eating raw food for one year, she dropped to 155 lbs and has stayed at that weight ever since. Bitte had to take Pravachol in 2002 because of her high cholesterol, which she had been subsequently taking for several years. After 10 months of eating raw food, Bitte stopped taking Pravachol completely, after consulting her doctor and undergoing a three-month trial period.

I took new tests in May 2008 which showed that I was healthy, and that my cholesterol levels were low.

Other positive effects of the raw food diet include smoother skin, and much less pain in her thumb joints. But above everything else, it is the increased energy that makes her stick with raw food.

When I was working, I noticed that I had much more energy and could interact more fully with my students, who are extremely lively. After work, I didn't just go home and rest, which is so easy to do when you are tired. Instead, I started to go on walks regularly after work, which in turn gave me even more energy.

Bitte, now retired, is still very active. She uses her energy for, among other things, local political events and spending time with her friends. She also works out twice a week at home.

I am going to continue with raw food for the rest of my life!

Erica's tips for a smooth transition to raw food:
1. Eat vegetarian food for several weeks before you eat only raw.
2. Remove the white ingredients—flour, sugar, and dairy products—from your diet.
3. Eat steamed vegetables, oven-baked root vegetables, cooked quinoa, couscous, and bulghur with your salads in the beginning.
4. Try eating only raw foods for 1 to 3 days. If it works for you, then try eating only raw for a longer period of time.

Don't forget:
- Eat until you are comfortably full.
- Eat regularly.
- Always have an "emergency bag" full of nuts, seeds, and dried fruit on hand.
- Drink approximately 8 cups of water a day.
- Drink herbal teas.
- When you are out or eating with friends, choose the best available alternative to raw (don't stress about it!).
- You can always eat a "first dinner" if you are invited over to a friend's house.
- Explain to your friends about raw food and why you are eating it.
- Be physically active every day.

basic recipes

A GOOD PLACE TO START

Bases are common ingredients in many recipes, but they can also be equally functional on their own. I recommend making a large batch and storing the extra in your refrigerator. These milks and dressings will last for approximately two days in the refrigerator, and the nut butters will stay fresh for about two weeks.

Raw Tahini

Most stores only sell tahini that is made from roasted sesame seeds. Even though you can find raw tahini in some health food stores, it is easy and much cheaper to make it at home. Have some ready-made tahini in your kitchen, as it makes a perfect base for dressings, smoothies and desserts.

½ cup raw sesame seeds
¼ cup canola or flaxseed oil
Sea salt, if desired

Blend the sesame seeds in a blender. Add a mild-flavored oil, such as canola or flaxseed, until you achieve a consistency like peanut butter. Add a little sea salt if desired. The tahini shouldn't be dry or oily, but somewhere in between.

Nut and Seed Butter

You can make nut and seed butters from any kind of nut or seed you want. Blend to a flour-like consistency in a blender and add a mild-flavored oil, like canola oil. The consistency should be like peanut butter. Nut butter makes a good butter substitute, and it works well as a base ingredient in dressings, smoothies, and desserts.

Pumpkin Seed Dressing

Another delicious base recipe. Experiment with your favorite herbs, or just use the ones that you have at home.

¼ cup pumpkin seeds
¼ bell pepper, yellow or red
½ teaspoon tarragon, sage, or another herb
1 teaspoon tamari
Lemon juice, to taste
¼ cup water

1. Blend all of the ingredients in the blender, adding water until you have a creamy consistency.
2. Season with extra tamari and lemon juice, if desired.

Walnut Dressing

You can make endless variations of this dressing. For example, try different colored bell peppers, remove the celery, and/or add other spices (dried or fresh).

¼ cup walnuts, soaked
½ red bell pepper
1 tablespoon lemon juice
1 teaspoon tamari
Basil, to taste
1 celery stalk, chopped
¼ cup water

1. Blend the walnuts to a flour-like consistency using a blender.
2. Add the remaining ingredients and pulse.
3. Add extra water to get the desired consistency. Season with extra basil, tamari and lemon juice if desired.

Ranch Dressing

Creamy and delicious dressing. Using this as a base, you can add your favorite mustard or spices to create new dressings.

½ cup cashew nuts
½ cup water
½ sprig of basil
½ sprig of dill
1 tablespoon lemon juice
Pinch of salt

1. Blend the cashews to a flour-like consistency using a blender.
2. Add half of the water, and mix.
3. Add the spices, lemon juice, and salt.
4. Add a little water at a time and blend until desired consistency.

Almond Milk

Almond milk is delicious, extremely nutritious, and very filling. You can make all sorts of varieties using dates, honey, berries, fruits, and spices. You can either soak and sprout the almonds, or use them straight from the bag.

1 cup almonds
2 cups water

1. Thoroughly blend ¾ cup of water with the almonds in a blender.
2. Pour the mixture (a little at a time) through a strainer, into a bowl below.
3. Use the back of a spoon to press the remaining liquid out of the mixture.
4. Blend the remaining mixture one more time to see if you get any extra milk. Save the leftover pulp to use in other recipes; it will last for about 1 day in the refrigerator.
5. Add a little more water to the milk and blend until desired consistency. If you use sprouted almonds, you can remove the almond shell by rinsing the nuts in lukewarm water, and removing the shell with your fingers.

Sesame Milk

Au naturel, or with banana, dates or honey. Sesame milk makes a perfect snack.

¼–½ cup raw sesame seeds
¾–1 ¼ cups water
Date, honey, or banana, if desired

1. Blend the sesame seeds to a flour-like consistency using a blender.
2. Add water until you have a milky consistency. Blend.
3. Add a date, honey, or some of a banana, if desired, and briefly blend.

Brazilian Milk

½ cup of Brazil nuts makes a large and satisfying glass of milk. Brazil nut milk is more filling, and has a richer taste, than almond milk.

½ cup Brazil nuts, soaked for 8 to 12 hours
1–1 ½ cups water
½ teaspoon vanilla powder or paste
1 teaspoon honey

1. Soak the Brazil nuts.
2. Thoroughly blend the nuts and ½ cup of water, using a blender.
3. Put the mixture (a little at a time) into a strainer, with the blender underneath. Use the back side of a spoon to press all of the liquid out of the mixture.
4. Add ¾ cup of water or more to the liquid in the blender, stirring by hand until desired consistency.
5. Add the vanilla and honey, and blend.

Pear Cashew Cream

You can also use real organic vanilla from the bean, which makes this taste even better.

1 cup cashews
1 very ripe, large pear, chopped
2 tablespoons water
1 teaspoon vanilla powder or paste

1. Blend the cashew nuts to a flour-like consistency using a blender.
2. Add the pear and water, and blend.
3. Blend until creamy, adding more water if needed. Add the vanilla and blend again.

TIP!
Freeze and in a few hours your pear cashew cream becomes a delectable ice cream.

Cashew Cream

This is another variation of raw cream, with no pear and extra almonds. Find your own favorite variation!

1 cup cashew nuts
¼ cup water
1 handful of almonds, soaked
½ or 1 vanilla bean
3 tablespoons canola oil, or flaxseed oil

1. Blend the cashews to a flour-like consistency using a blender.
2. Add 2 tablespoons of water and the almonds, and blend again.
3. Start by adding half of the vanilla bean, using the whole bean and not just the seeds. Add the oil, and blend.
4. Add the rest of the vanilla bean and/or more water, if desired.

Sour Cream Cheese

Season this cheese with garlic, chives, and your favorite spices and herbs. Good in combination with flaxseed crackers, or on a salad sandwich.

1 cup cashew nuts
½ cup water
1 ½ tablespoons lemon juice
Salt, to taste
2 inches of a leek
1 tablespoon fresh basil
1 tablespoon fresh dill

1. Put all of the ingredients in a food processor and blend thoroughly. Transfer mixture to a serving bowl.
2. Let the mixture cool in the refrigerator before serving. Lasts for 5 days in the fridge.

Cashew and Cauliflower Mash

This dish is reminiscent of a creamy soft cheese. Tastes delicious as is, but also good with fresh herbs, cumin, or other spices.

½ cup cashew nuts
½ cauliflower head, cut into smaller pieces
1 tablespoon olive oil
1 teaspoon sea salt
Choose your own spices and/or herbs

1. Put the nuts and cauliflower separately in the food processor, and blend until finely chopped.
2. Now put both the nuts and the cauliflower in the food processor. Add the olive oil and salt, and blend thoroughly.
3. Add the spices and/or herbs of your choice, and blend a little more.

Gingerbread Cookies

6 COOKIES

Who hasn't eaten up most of the gingerbread dough before baking it?! Here is a raw variation that tastes similar to gingerbread cookies. Get out your favorite cookie cutters and make these cookies, but don't bake the dough!

½ cup almonds
½ tablespoon almond oil or canola oil
2 dates
1 teaspoon cinnamon
½ teaspoon ginger
6 cloves, ground, or 1 teaspoon cloves, in powder form
Pinch of salt
1 tablespoon honey

TIP!
You can also roll the dough into balls.

1. Mix the almonds to a flour-like consistency, using a food processor.
2. Add the oil and dates. Mix.
3. Add the spices and salt, and mix again. Taste to make sure the spices are evenly spread out throughout the mixture.
4. Add the honey, and blend until the mixture has a consistency like gingerbread dough. Spread/roll the dough out on a cutting board, and make your cookies!

Every Occasion Balls

12 BALLS

These balls are one of my favorites to make, regardless of the occasion. The first reaction I typically get is "Are we going to eat meatballs for dessert?" They may look like meatballs, but they certainly don't taste like them!

1½ cups walnuts
¾ cup raisins
1 tablespoon honey
1½ tablespoons carob powder
Pinch of salt
Coconut flakes, for rolling

1. Place the walnuts in a food processor and pulse until finely chopped.
2. Add the raisins and mix thoroughly.
3. Add the honey, carob, and salt, and mix again. Add a little extra carob if you want a stronger chocolate taste.
4. Keep mixing until the dough holds together enough so it easy to roll balls. You can also roll the balls in coconut flakes.

Lasts for a week in the refrigerator and also keeps in the freezer.

1 Cashew Balls with Lime and Coconut

Snacks with a zing.

1 cup cashew nuts
½ cup raisins
Pinch of salt
Zest from 1 lime
1 or 2 tablespoons lemon juice
Coconut flakes, for rolling

1. Coarsely chop the cashew nuts in a food processor.
2. Add the raisins and mix until the ingredients congeal.
3. Add the salt, lime zest, and lemon juice.
4. Mix thoroughly.
5. Roll the dough into balls, and roll them in coconut flakes.

5 Trail Mix Balls

These will keep you full for a long time.

¼ cup raisins
4 dates
5 figs
6 apricots
¼ cup sunflower seeds
Coconut flakes or whole sunflower seeds, for rolling

1. Pulse the sunflower seeds in the food processor until they are coarsely chopped.
2. Add the dried fruit. Blend until everything is thoroughly mixed, and roll the resulting dough into balls.
3. Roll the balls in coconut or whole sunflower seeds.

2 Licorice Balls

Licorice was something I really missed when I started eating raw food. I screamed for joy in my kitchen when I finally found that taste that I was longing for.

1 cup tahini (see recipe p. 132)
4 tablespoons black sesame seeds, ground
Pinch of sea salt
4 teaspoons carob powder
2½ teaspoons anise
Whole black sesame seeds, for rolling

1. Blend all the ingredients in a bowl. Use a little more or less carob and anise, depending on your taste preferences.
2. Roll the balls in the whole sesame seeds.

3 Tahini Balls

Candy full of calcium, protein and energy.

2 tablespoons tahini (see recipe p. 132)
1 tablespoon honey
2 teaspoons carob powder
Pinch of salt
Coconut flakes or sesame seeds, for rolling

1. In a bowl, mix all the ingredients—except for the carob—together by hand.
2. Add the carob powder, using more or less depending on your taste preferences.
3. Roll the balls in coconut flakes or sesame seeds.

4 Ginger and Cinnamon Balls

These give you a quick energy boost.

4 dried figs
4 fresh dates
½ cup walnuts
½ cup raisins
¼ inch of fresh ginger, peeled
½ tablespoon cinnamon
Juice from ½ of a lime
Chopped walnuts, for rolling

1. Put the ingredients in a food processor, and mix until it becomes like dough.
2. Add extra lime, ginger and cinnamon if desired.
3. Make small balls, and roll them in walnuts.
4. Freeze the extras, and you've got a quick fix for the next time you want something sweet.

desserts

YUM-YUM FOR THE BODY!

Treat yourself and eat these desserts as snacks, a tea-time sweet treat, or even as a lazy Sunday morning breakfast. After all, these recipes contain only delicious natural ingredients, which give you energy and nourishment.

Raspberry Pie with Chocolate Sauce

Raspberries and chocolate are always a winning combination!

¼ cup hazelnuts
2 figs, soaked
2 dates
2 teaspoons honey
Pinch of salt
Soaking water from the figs
1 cup or more raspberries

Chocolate Sauce:
2 tablespoons carob or raw cocoa
2 tablespoons water
Pinch of salt
1 teaspoon honey

1. Blend the hazelnuts in the food processor until they are finely chopped.
2. Add the figs, dates, honey, and salt. Mix to form a dough.
3. Add a little of the soaking water, if needed.
4. Spread the dough in a pie pan, just like you would a regular pie crust. Place the raspberries in as filling.
5. Blend the sauce ingredients together. Chill before serving.
6. When serving, pour the sauce over the pie, and enjoy!

Chocolate Sauce

You never know when those chocolate cravings will strike; that's why it's always a good idea to have this sauce ready to go in the refrigerator. Try adding finely chopped figs or pecan nuts to the sauce, right before serving.

½ cup tahini
3 tablespoons honey
¼ cup water
5 tablespoons carob powder

1. By hand, mix all of the ingredients—except for the carob powder—together in a bowl.
2. Add the carob and mix again. This lasts for about a month in the fridge.

> **TIP!**
> Smoothie recipe: mix 3 tbs. honey, 2 tbs. tahini, 2 tbs. carob powder, and some water in a blender.

Nut Pie

4 PORTIONS

This nutty pie will keep in the fridge (wrapped in plastic) for about a week. Good to have ready-made for those unexpected guests, or simply when you want a delicious dessert.

Crust:
¼ cup almonds
¼ cup pecans
½ cup walnuts
Pinch of salt
½ teaspoon vanilla powder
½ cup dates
1 tablespoon honey

Filling:
6 dates
½ cup macadamia nuts or Brazil nuts
1 tablespoon honey
½ avocado
½ teaspoon cinnamon
½ teaspoon ginger
Pinch of nutmeg

1. To make the crust: put the nuts in the food processor and pulse until finely chopped.
2. Add the rest of the crust ingredients and mix.
3. Spread the dough out in a pie pan.
4. Blend the filling ingredients together in a food processor.
5. Spread the filling out inside the pie crust.
6. Serve the pie as is, or with some fruit, berries, or cashew cream on the side.

Raw Cheesecake

2 PORTIONS

Add some coconut for a sweeter taste.

1¼ cups macadamia nuts, soaked
½ cup Brazil nuts, soaked
Juice from ½ of a lemon
2 teaspoons honey
Pinch of salt
½ cup raspberries

1. Soak the nuts for at least 2 hours.
2. Blend the nuts in a food processor, until finely chopped.
3. Add the lemon juice, honey, and salt, and blend again.
4. Serve with fresh or thawed raspberries.

Apple Pie

4 PORTIONS

You only have to try this once to be sold on raw apple pie!

Crust:
1¾ cups almonds
1 tablespoon canola oil or almond oil
5 fresh dates
Pinch of nutmeg
2 teaspoons cinnamon
Pinch of salt
1 tablespoon honey

Filling:
1 or 2 apples
1 banana
2 dates
1 teaspoon cinnamon

Garnish:
2 or 3 apples, sliced
Cinnamon, to taste

1. Finely chop the nuts in a food processor.
2. Add the oil, dates, spices, and salt. Mix.
3. Add the honey, and mix to form a dough.
4. Spread the dough out on the bottom of a pie dish.
5. Thoroughly blend the filling ingredients in a food processor, and place inside the pie.
6. Garnish with sliced apples. Sprinkle cinnamon on top.

Peach Pie

You can also use nectarines. The taste is a little different, but equally delicious.

Crust:
1¾ cup almonds
Pinch of salt
1 teaspoon cinnamon
Pinch of nutmeg
4 dates
2 tablespoons honey
1 or 2 tablespoons almond or canola oil

Filling:
4 peaches, sliced
Pinch of salt
Pinch of nutmeg
1 teaspoon cinnamon
1 tablespoon coconut flakes
4 dates
1 tablespoon honey
Mint or lemon balm, for garnishing

1. Finely chop the almonds in a food processor.
2. Add the rest of the crust ingredients, and mix thoroughly.
3. Spread the dough out evenly on the bottom of a pie dish.
4. Put 2 peaches in a food processor. When they are finely chopped, add the rest of the filling ingredients, except for the last 2 peaches. Blend thoroughly, and remove from food processor.
5. Put the remaining 2 sliced peaches in the filling mixture. Stir by hand.
6. Pour the filling into the pie dish.
7. Garnish with fresh mint or lemon balm.

Mango Lemon Balm Ice Cream

You can use fresh or frozen mango. Buy fresh mangoes when they are on sale, chop them up, and freeze.

1 mango, fresh or frozen
1 banana, frozen
Lemon balm, chopped

1. Let the banana and frozen mango thaw for about 10 minutes.
2. Break the banana into pieces and put the pieces and the mango into a food processor.
3. Blend until smooth.
4. Garnish with lemon balm. Serve immediately.

Nectarine Ice Cream

Frozen banana makes a great base for a variety of fruit and berry ice cream flavors. Nectarine is one yummy alternative; raspberries are another winner. Even adding a couple of dates to the banana mixture does a lot.

1 nectarine, chopped
1 banana, frozen

1. Thaw the banana for about 10 minutes.
2. Break the banana into pieces and put the pieces and the nectarine into a food processor.
3. Blend until smooth.
4. Serve with golden flaxseed crackers (p. 116).

Brownies

6 PORTIONS

For another brownie variation, substitute tahini for the almonds. Sprout the almonds if you want, or use them straight out of the bag.

¾ cup almonds
¾ cup dates
1 tablespoon honey
1½ tablespoons carob powder
Pinch of salt
Cape gooseberry, if desired

1. Soak the almonds for 12 hours.
2. Remove the soaking water, and let the almonds sprout for 24 hours. Again, sprouting and soaking isn't necessary, but it does make the almonds easier to digest.
3. Chop the almonds in a food processor, or chop them by hand into small pieces.
4. Chop the dates in a food processor, or chop them by hand into small pieces.
5. Mix the dates and almonds together in a bowl.
6. Add the honey, carob powder, and salt, mixing the ingredients together by hand.
7. Spread out the mixture on to a baking pan, and put in the fridge for an hour before serving.
8. Serve with cape gooseberry, if desired. The sour taste of cape gooseberry is superb in combination with the sweetness of the brownies, and the fruit makes a beautiful garnish.

Chocolate and Banana Cake

Equally delicious as a dessert or snack. Use the remaining almond leftovers from making almond milk.

Almond leftovers from almond milk (from about ½ cup of almonds, or 1½ cups of milk)
1 tablespoon honey
Pinch of salt
Carob powder, to taste
1 banana, sliced

1. Blend the almonds, honey, salt, and carob—either in a blender or in a bowl—until you have the taste and consistency that you are happy with.
2. Place in a bowl or on a plate. If you are doubling the recipe, serve on a cake dish.
3. Garnish with banana slices.

Carrot Cake

4 PORTIONS

This was borne out of necessity, my own carrot cake cravings and lack of other ingredients in the kitchen!

Crust:
4 carrots
1 apple, coarsely grated
¼ cup almonds, finely chopped
4 fresh dates, finely chopped
1 teaspoon cinnamon
Pinch of nutmeg
3 tablespoons lemon zest

Garnish with:
Pear cashew cream (p. 139)
Raisins and/or walnuts, to taste

1. Finely grate the carrots. (You can also use the carrot "leftovers" from making carrot juice if you have these lying around).
2. Use a strainer to remove any excess juice from the carrots.
3. Mix the crust ingredients together in a bowl, by hand, or use a food processor.
4. Spread the crust out on a plate and put in the refrigerator until you are ready to serve.
5. When serving, spread a thick layer of pear cashew cream over the crust, and garnish with walnuts and raisins.

Coconut Carrot Cake

4 PORTIONS

This carrot cake isn't as sweet as many of the other desserts, and it tastes even better after a day in the refrigerator.

Crust:
4 carrots
4 fresh dates
¼ cup coconut
Juice from ½ of a lemon
2 tablespoons lemon zest

Topping:
½ cup pine nuts
1 apricot, soaked
1 tablespoon of apricot soaking water
Splash of lime juice

1. Finely grate the carrots.
2. Use a strainer to remove any excess liquid from the carrots.
3. Mix the crust ingredients together in a food processor. It may take a couple of minutes. Spread the crust out in a cake or pie dish and place in the refrigerator.
4. Blend the pine nuts to a flour-like consistency using a blender or food processor.
5. Add a little of the soaking water to the mixture while blending, until it becomes creamy. Add the apricot and blend again.
6. Add a splash of lime juice and blend again. Place the topping on the crust, and chill for about an hour before serving.

Raw Pie Crust

4 PORTIONS

This is the raw version of your standard pie crust, which you can fill with all sorts of berries and fruits. One of my favorites is blueberry pie and cashew cream with a little vanilla. Yum!

2 cups walnuts
¾ cup coconut flakes
½ teaspoon cinnamon
½ teaspoon nutmeg
Pinch of salt
8 dates
½ cup raisins
1–2 tablespoons honey

Suggestions for Fillings:
blueberries, raspberries, strawberries, or blackberries, fresh or thawed.

1. Mix the walnuts, coconut and spices in the food processor until the walnuts are finely chopped.
2. Add the dates, raisins, and honey. Mix until mixture is similar to dough.
3. Lay out the dough in a pie dish and fill with berries of your choice. Thawed berries give the pie crust a more gooey consistency, because the juice from the thawing berries soaks into the crust. The crust keeps for 1 week in the fridge and 3 months in the freezer.

Fluffy Chocolate Mousse

2 PORTIONS

This is good in combination with raw cheesecake and/or with raspberries on the side. If you want a true chocolate taste for your mousse and you can't find raw cocoa, you can always "cheat" a little and use the roasted cocoa.

¼ cup dates
¼–½ cup water
2 tablespoons honey
½ teaspoon vanilla powder
¾ cup avocado
¼ cup cocoa or carob powder

1. Blend the dates, ¼ cup water, honey, and vanilla in a food processor until the mixture is soft.
2. Add the avocado and the cocoa or carob. Blend until creamy. Stop now and again and scrape the mixture off the sides of the food processor.
3. Add a little more water for a thinner consistency. Lasts for about 3 days in the fridge, and 2 weeks in the freezer (store in a sealed container).

Nutty Carob Mousse

2 PORTIONS

Rich and satisfying.

½ cup cashew nuts
¼ cup pine nuts
½ cup almonds
3 dates
2 tablespoons water
3 tablespoons carob or cocoa powder
1 avocado

Serve with:
Honey
Coconut flakes

1. Blend the nuts in a food processor until finely chopped.
2. Add the dates, water, and carob or cocoa, and blend again.
3. Add the avocado and blend.
4. Serve the mousse after it has chilled for an hour in the refrigerator.
5. Garnish with a little honey and coconut flakes.

Simply Luxurious

Luxury doesn't have to mean that it's complicated!

1 pear, chopped
4 fresh dates, chopped
7 walnuts, coarsely chopped

Stir all ingredients in a bowl, and enjoy.

Nectarine and Strawberry Smoothie

2 PORTIONS

A refreshing drink for those sweltering summer days.

Juice from 1 orange
¼ cup water
2 nectarines, cut into pieces
15 strawberries, fresh or frozen
1 tablespoon honey

1. Blend the orange juice, water, and nectarine pieces in a blender.
2. Add the strawberries a few at a time, and blend again.
3. Add the honey, and drink!

The Vitai-Cederholm family consists of 43-year-old Frank Vitai, 30-year-old Carola Cederholm, and children Cindy, 18; Oskar, 11; and 9-year-old Emilie. They live in Hässleholm, Sweden. Sandra, 20 years old, no longer lives at home.

Carola works as a therapist and Frank as a kinesthesiologist. In their spare time, the family enjoys spending time together, relaxing and playing games. Swimming in lakes or the ocean is another group favorite. Carola and Frank also enjoy working out: "When it comes to being healthy, working out is just as important as diet."

Frank's favorite raw food tips for families with children: "First, be aware of your own diet and what food means to you. Work on changing your own habits first. Parents are teachers, and children do what we do—not what we say."

children

BECOME INTERESTED IN FOOD WHEN THEY SEE ADULTS WHO ENJOY EATING.

The Vitai-Cederholm Family eats progressively more and more raw food.

Mornings begin with fresh fruit and vegetables. The Vitai-Cederholm family enjoy their latest juice creation: orange, apple, pear, and carrots, plus a little lime and fresh ginger. There are always bowls full of nuts and dried fruits out, so the kids can snack on them whenever they like between meals.

"The bowls become empty very quickly; it's probably a sign that the fruit and nuts are appreciated," says Frank with a laugh.

Frank Vitae and Carola Cederholm have been together for three years. Two years ago, they moved in together and created a new family with their children Cindy, Oskar and Emilie. Good food and a healthy lifestyle were important for both Frank and Carola even before they met. Frank has been on this path for a long time; when he was only eight years old, he stopped eating sugar because he had a fear of going to the dentist. He hasn't eaten meat for 20 years. Carola has now stopped eating sugar and is also vegetarian.

"Raw food was introduced to our family because of our friendship with Erica. When she came to visit us, she brought tons of fresh, raw foods that she trans-formed into delicious meals," explains Frank. "I became fascinated by the idea that it is possible to prepare a fantastic meal without having to cook the food."

The family has doubled their intake of raw food within the last year. More than anything else, they eat extra salads, making them more filling and exciting by adding nuts, flaxseed, buckwheat, quinoa, and sprouts.

On special occasions, they make their favorite dish, one of Erica's raw food pies. The crust is made of nuts, coconut, honey, and cinnamon; the filling consists of blue-berries and raspberries. Served with cashew cream, this pie always impresses and surprises their guests. Frank says: "They can't believe it tastes so good without sugar or other unhealthy ingredients!"

Frank and Carola openly discuss with their children how different types of food and diet affect people, and which foods they think are healthy. However, these dis-cussions are always casual, and they let their children decide for themselves how they want to eat. One of their kids eats meat occasionally, and all of the kids have eaten candy and sweets from time to time.

Frank strongly believes that the most important aspect of helping children change their diet for the better is to be a positive role model through eating healthy foods yourself. "My experience is that children naturally want to be a part of the family and copy what the parents do," explains Frank.

"Carola and I love food, and our kids become interested because they see how delicious we think it is!"

On two occasions, the Vitai-Cederholm family has eaten solely raw food as part of a detox, and they feel that it is soon time for a third. Their detox consists of eating only raw food for three days, and eliminating salt from their diet, in order to make it as easy as possible for the body to get rid of waste products.

"Although we always eat healthily and feel good, we feel even better after eating only raw food. Even on the third day, you feel lighter and more energetic. It is a similar feeling to when one stops eating meat and starts eating only vegetarian food. My 18-year-old daughter Cindy has also experienced this."

"The only negative aspect of eating more raw food is that some products are expensive, like cashew nuts, for example. There isn't as big a selection of nuts, fruits and vegetables here in Hässelholm as you would find in larger cities. Hopefully, this will change."

Frank thinks that the best part of eating raw food is that food plays a more central role in your everyday life: "You are automatically more connected to what you are eating and have a more natural relationship with food."

"I believe that, more and more, people are returning back to the basics. In the past, there wasn't another alternative and you ate what was available, but now we understand that eating natural, raw food is necessary. But it is equally important that it tastes delicious; children would never eat something just because it is nutritious!"

Erica and Irmela's tips for families that want to increase their daily intake of raw food:

- Educate yourself—it is important to know if your children are getting all the nutrients they need in order to grow and develop properly.
- Serve the food in a creative or attractive manner, so children become interested.
- Add a raw food side dish to the food that your children already regularly eat.
- Food preferences are deeply connected to habit. Allow your kids to try the same food several times before giving up on it.
- When your kids are hungry for snacks, or waiting for a meal to be ready, give them bite-sized pieces of fresh vegetables—for example, carrots, lettuce leaves, cucumber, cauliflower and cabbage—to snack on.
- Have a bowl of nuts, seeds and dried fruit easily available so the kids can snack on these when they feel like it.
- When the sweet cravings start, offer a raw dessert instead of a baked one.
- Serve raw food when you have guests for dinner. The more people eating the food the better, as children become inspired through others' appreciation.
- Make some yummy raw food snacks together with your children, and eat them as a weekend treat. This turns raw food into a fun activity, and it always tastes better when you have made it yourself!

nutritional information

Eating raw food prompts a lot of curiosity and questions, the most common being: where do you get your protein, how many calories do you eat, where are the carbs, and how do you get enough vitamins and minerals? Here are brief answers to some of these questions.

There are many different opinions, advice and findings out there, but only you can decide how you feel and how raw food works for you. Listen to expert advice, but also listen to and trust your own body and its inherent intelligence.

My experience is that people who eat raw food for longer periods of time automatically become more in tune with their body. For example, they start to crave the foods that contain the nutrients their body needs.

What you stop eating can often be more important than what you do eat. For example, if you increase your intake of fruits and vegetables while continuing to eat the food that makes you feel tired, you won't notice too much of a change in your overall well-being. Think about those foods that seem to "steal" your energy; more often than not, these are the foods that we often consume, but—for one reason or another—tend to forget that we eat.

Always choose the best available alternative, in each passing moment.

Where Do I Get My:

Protein
There is protein, albeit in very small quantities, in almost every vegetable and fruit. The most protein-rich raw food sources are seeds, nuts, almonds, certain grains, and sprouts. For example, 3 ½ ounces of dried lentils contains 20 grams of protein. Protein functions like building blocks in our bodies, as we need it in order to build and maintain muscle. Protein contains amino acids. Of the 20 amino acids, eight of them are essential, meaning we need to ingest them via the food we eat, and 12 of them are so-called non-essential, which means that the body produces them on its own.

Carbohydrates
Carbohydrates are the body and brain's most important source of fuel. Carbohydrates are converted into glucose, which in turn provides energy for our cells. There are so-called simple and complex carbohydrates. In these carb-fixated times, we are often told that all carbohydrates are dangerous, that is, if you want to be thin and have stable blood sugar levels. This is true, but only to a certain extent. One will naturally be unhealthy and feel bad if one eats too many simple carbs (i.e., white bread, sugar, and soda); however, humans need to eat complex carbs in order to survive.

Almost every ingredient in raw food contains slow carbohydrates. The major exception is dried fruit, which can be classified as fast carbohydrates. One shared characteristic of comples carbs is that they contain more roughage than their simple counterparts. Roughage helps ensure that our intestines are up to par and that we have a stable blood sugar level throughout the day. Fruit, vegetables, and grains all contain carbohydrates.

Fat

We need fat in order to survive! Fat is required for the normal production of certain hormones in the body and for protecting our inner organs. Fat also functions as a sort of fuel for the brain. However, too much of anything is never healthy, especially unhealthy fats that clog up our arteries and make us lethargic. Unhealthy fat sources include dairy products, animal products and fried food.

Through eating nuts and seeds, raw food provides the healthy types of fats that our bodies need. We should still make sure that we eat a reasonable amount of these foods, and that the oil we use is cold pressed. The fruit highest in fat is the avocado, and the nut highest in fat is the macadamia nut.

Vitamins and Minerals

Many people think of vitamin and nutrient supplements when they hear the words vitamins and minerals, instead of the actual food that we eat. Vitamins and minerals are essential, meaning that we need them in order to live. Because we don't produce these naturally in our bodies, we must get our required supply from the foods that we eat. We need vitamins and minerals for the health and maintenance of our many different biochemical and physiological bodily processes, such as hormone regulation and metabolism. We also need vitamins and minerals in order to maintain a healthy skeleton.

The vitamins and minerals that are most discussed within raw food are listed in this paragraph. First, vitamin B_{12}: It is recommended to take a vitamin B_{12} supplement if you only eat raw food, to ensure that you are receiving enough of this vitamin. Vitamin B_6 is needed for metabolizing protein in the body; bananas, avocados and nuts are all good sources of Vitamin B_6. Vitamins A, C, and E are necessary for many reasons, one of them being that they function as antioxidants. You can find these vitamins in all sorts of fruits and vegetables. The best raw sources of vitamin E are nuts, seeds, avocados, almonds, and grains. A good rule of thumb is that the darker the fruit or vegetable's color, the greater the amount of antioxidants. Air pollution, environmental pollutants, stimulants and other drugs, and stress are some of the many reasons why many of us have more free radicals in our bodies than humans did in the past. Free radicals influence the aging process and harm our bodies' cells; antioxidants help prevent this from happening.

Zinc—is needed for over 200 different enzyme-related processes in the body, and it also plays an important role in maintaining a healthy immune system. Zinc is an antioxidant and thus helps prevent cell damage. Zinc is also connected to one's sex drive. The best raw food sources of zinc are pumpkin seeds, sunflower seeds and parsley.

Calcium—plays an important role in building a strong skeleton, and having strong teeth. Raw foods rich in calcium are dark leafy greens, sesame seeds and nuts.

Folic acid—decreases the risk for fetal developmental problems, and can improve men's sperm quality. Nuts, bananas and leafy greens are rich in folic acid.

Iron—is needed to build red blood cells. We also need vitamin C in order to absorb iron effectively. You can find iron in, among other foods, dried apricots, strawberries and leafy greens.

Why Do We Need Water?

We need water for many reasons, one being that it maintains the health of the cells in our bodies. We also need water for many other vital processes in the body, including transportation of nutrients and waste products. We can live for quite a while without food, but we will only survive for a couple of days without water.

Adults consist of 60% water. A newborn consists of 80% water. How much water should you drink a day? If you are moderately physically active, between 1 and 2 liters of water a day should be fine, as you also absorb liquid through the food that you eat.

One excellent aspect of raw food is that your body naturally receives liquid through your large intake of vegetables and fruits. Symptoms of dehydration are sugar cravings, lethargy, headaches, constipation, and dry skin.

inspirational books

Cohen, Alissa. *Living on Live Food*. Laguna Beach: Cohen, 2004.

Cornbleet, Jennifer. *Raw Food Made Easy*. Summertown: Book Publishing Company, 2005.

Dorit. *Celebrating Our Raw Nature*. Summertown: Book Publishing Company, 2007.

Juliano & Lenkert, Erica. *RAW the UNcook Book*. New York: HarperCollins Publishers, 1999.

Melngailis, Sarma; et. al. *Raw Food Real World*. New York: ReganBooks, 2005.

Stokes, Angela. *RawReform: How to Go Raw for Weight Loss*. Raw Vegan books.

Wolfe, David. *The Sunfood Diet Success System*. Aliso Viejo: Maul Brothers Publishing, 2006.

resources

The organic raw foods available in your area are highly dependent, of course, on where you live. Even if you live in a small town, finding affordable raw food may not be as difficult as you think. The majority of grocery stores now carry organic produce, and natural food stores are increasing in popularity. Don't forget that it doesn't take much money, space, or effort to start your very own organic garden right at home! There are also many online resources available that offer a wide selection of information, food, and products all related to raw food. Some of these resources are listed here.

LOCAL RESOURCES

Farmers Markets are steadily increasing in number across the country. Almost every major city has farmers markets, as do many other smaller communities. This is a great place to go to buy local, organic produce. The staff is usually very knowledgeable and can tell you all about which fruits and veggies are in season.

Natural Food Stores often carry harder-to-find raw food products, such as agave nectar, goji berries, and spirulina. For a cheaper and more environmentally friendly alternative, purchase your raw grains and nuts from the bulk bins instead of buying them pre-packaged. Staff members can help you with special orders.

CSA (Community Supported Agriculture) is another way to get local, organic produce directly from a farmer. Usually you purchase a share or a membership, and receive a weekly box of produce during the farming season. Go to www.localharvest.org/csa for more information and to find a CSA near you.

ONLINE RESOURCES

www.rawfoods.com
An informative website all about raw food. If you click on City Search, or go to www.rawfoods.com/cityguide you can search for local farmers markets, raw food restaurants, natural food stores, and other similar places of interest in your neighborhood.

www.sunfood.com
For ordering non-perishable raw food.

www.therawfoodworld.com
For ordering raw food and appliances.

www.rawguru.com
For ordering bulk perishable and non-perishable raw food, and appliances.

Author Contact Information

Erica Palmcrantz Aziz, raw food educator.
Contact: www.rawfoodbyerica.com